ORTHO'S All About

Houseplants

Written by Kate Jerome

Meredith® Books
Des Moines, Iowa

Ortho® Books
An imprint of Meredith® Books

All About Houseplants
Editor: Marilyn Rogers
Contributing Editor: Leona H. Openshaw
Contributing Technical Editors: Elvin McDonald,
   Darrell Trout
Art Director: Tom Wegner
Copy Chief: Catherine Hamrick
Copy and Production Editor: Terri Fredrickson
Contributing Copy Editors: Cynthia S. Howell, Ed Malles,
   Carol Boker, James A. Baggett
Contributing Proofreaders: Kathy Roth Eastman, Mary Pas,
   Margaret Smith
Contributing Illustrators: Pam Wattenmaker,
   Cyndie Wooley
Contributing Prop/Photo Stylist: Peggy Johnston
Indexer: Don Glassman
Electronic Production Coordinator: Paula Forest
Editorial and Design Assistants: Kathleen Stevens,
   Karen Schirm
Production Director: Douglas M. Johnston
Production Manager: Pam Kvitne
Assistant Prepress Manager: Marjorie J. Schenkelberg

Additional Editorial Contributions from
   Art Rep Services
Director: Chip Nadeau
Designer: lk Design
Illustrator: Shawn Wallace

Meredith® Books
Editor in Chief: James D. Blume
Design Director: Matt Strelecki
Managing Editor: Gregory H. Kayko
Executive Ortho Editor: Benjamin W. Allen

Director, Sales & Marketing, Retail: Michael A. Peterson
Director, Sales & Marketing, Special Markets:
   Rita McMullen
Director, Sales & Marketing, Home & Garden Center
   Channel: Ray Wolf
Director, Operations: George A. Susral
Vice President, General Manager: Jamie L. Martin

Meredith Publishing Group
President, Publishing Group: Christopher M. Little
Vice President, Consumer Marketing & Development:
   Hal Oringer

Meredith Corporation
Chairman and Chief Executive Officer: William T. Kerr
Chairman of the Executive Committee: E.T. Meredith III

Thanks to
Janet Anderson, Mary Bendgen, Katelyn Buckton,
Nick Buckton, Katherine Dickson, Amelia Dohlman,
Michelle George, Melissa George, Lori Gould, Gina Hale,
Dave Kvitne, Aimee Reiman, Ashley Rench,
Andrew Robinson, Audra Robinson, Mary Irene Swartz;
Floorcraft Nursery, San Francisco, Calif.

Photographers
(Photographers credited may retain copyright ©
   to the listed photographs.)
L= Left, R= Right, C= Center, B= Bottom, T= Top
Laurie A. Black: p. 12;
Patricia Bruno/Positive Images: p. 53(BR);
Crandall & Crandall: p. 6(R), 10(C);
Alan & Linda Detrick: p. 5(B), 9(T), 24(TR), 46(TR),
   49(B), 55(T);
Derek Fell: p. 5(TR);
Charles Marden Fitch: p. 44(B), 49(T);
John Glover: p. 3T, 9(B);
David Goldberg: p. 53(T), 55(B);
John Holtorf: p. 3(B), 58–59;
Jerry Howard/Positive Images: p. 50(T);
Elvin McDonald: p. 11(TL), 57;
Jerry Pavia: p. 11(TR), 20(L);
Pam Peirce: p. 46(BL);
Susan A. Roth: p. 11(RC);
Richard Shiell: p. 47(TR);
Joseph G. Strauch, Jr.: p. 48(B);
The Studio Central: p. 6(L), 17, 26, 27, 28, 29, 30, 31, 32,
   33, 35, 36, 37, 38, 39, 41(L), 42, 43B, 52, Directory of
   Houseplants: p. 62–92;
Steve Struse: p. 8(T, BL), 14, 15, 20(R), 21, 22(C), 23(C),
   24(TL, BL, BR), 25, 40, 43(T), 50(B), 51(B), 53(BL), 54;
Michael S. Thompson: p. 3(C), 4, 5(TL), 10(T), 46(BR);
Connie Toops: p. 11(BL);
Ron West: p. 44(T), 47(BL, BR), 48(T), 51(T);

Note to the Readers: Due to differing conditions, tools,
and individual skills, Meredith Corporation assumes no
responsibility for any damages, injuries suffered, or losses
incurred as a result of following the information published
in this book. Before beginning any project, review the
instructions carefully. Always read and observe all of the
safety precautions provided by manufacturers of any
tools, equipment, or supplies, and follow all accepted
safety procedures.

Cover photograph: Steve Struse, Struse Photography

All of us at Ortho® Books are dedicated to providing you
with the information and ideas you need to enhance your
home and garden. We welcome your comments and
suggestions about this book. Write to us at:
   Meredith Corporation
   Ortho Books
   1716 Locust St.
   Des Moines, IA 50309–3023

If you would like more information on other Ortho
products, call 800-225-2883 or visit us at www.ortho.com

4

SUCCESS WITH HOUSEPLANTS

Although the world of houseplants does contain some prima donnas, most are as easy to grow as they are attractive. If the floral department at the grocery leaves you trembling in your boots for fear you'll bring home a truly difficult one, and yet you still yearn to fill your home with beautiful foliage and flowers, then read on. You can have a houseful of plants that won't overtax your resources. This book will teach you how to select plants to match your specific skill, time, and interest levels, as well as how to care for them with confidence.

You'll learn, too, that you don't necessarily need to limit yourself only to easy-care plants. To grow the vast majority of houseplants, all you need to do is master just a few simple cultural techniques.

A spotted dumb cane offers your setting a hint of tropical lushness. It's also strikingly easy to grow, given the right conditions—medium light and medium temperatures.

MAKING THE MATCH

Indoor gardeners tend to be divided into two groups: those who buy plants on impulse, hoping that their purchase will survive, and those who buy plants with the idea of making them a permanent addition to their home. If you fall into this latter group, you'll want to keep several points in mind as you shop.

LOCATION, LOCATION, LOCATION: First, take stock of the conditions in your home before you make a purchase. One of the most critical steps to ensuring the long-term health of indoor plants is being able to supply the kind of growing conditions they require. You will only be frustrated if you try to grow a plant in an unsuitable spot.

For example, if you want a houseplant for a south window, which receives hot sun all day all year long, buy a cactus, euphorbia, or other sun-loving plant instead of a more delicate, shade-loving African violet. On the other hand, if the spot receives only indirect, or medium, light, you will have poor luck with high-light plants, such as cactus and hibiscus. For an area with little light, you can create an

HARD-TO-KILL PLANTS

Chinese evergreen	Hoya, wax plant
Aloe, medicine plant	Split-leaf
Asparagus fern	philodendron
Aspidistra, cast-iron	Ponytail palm,
plant	elephant-foot tree
Umbrella plant	Sweet olive
Living-vase plant	Peperomia
Fishtail palm	Philodendron
Chamaedorea,	Artillery plant
bamboo palm	Swedish ivy
Old-man cactus	Lady palm
Spider plant	Snake plant
Dracaena	Cape primrose
Pothos, devil's ivy	Arrowhead vine
Japanese aralia	Wandering Jew
Ficus, fig	Purple wandering
English ivy	Jew

When surrounded by more subdued plants, a variegated weeping fig becomes a striking focal point.

Let camellia—with its large, perfectly formed blossoms—color your home. Keep in mind that the plant thrives best in a cool location or greenhouse, preferably with morning light from the east.

arresting display of foliage and flowers, using plants such as philodendron, peace lily, and pothos.

If you love the exhilaration of an open bedroom window during winter, you will be disappointed with the performance of grape ivy or anthurium, which do poorly in drafty areas. Instead, pick a fatsia or Norfolk Island pine, which tolerate cooler temperatures. If you have an enclosed porch that you don't heat in winter but it doesn't freeze, take advantage of it by selecting plants that need a cold, dormant period.

Whatever the climate in your home, the "Directory of Houseplants" (starting on page 58) will help you identify and select the best plants for your specific conditions.

COMPLEMENT YOUR STYLE: Second, consider how much room you have for houseplants. Have you ever seen a striking plant in a hotel lobby, office building, or conservatory and vowed that you would get one for your home? Then, when you visited a greenhouse, not only did the cost take your breath away but you also realized that the plant's size would dwarf everything else in the house. Instead, think beforehand about the scale of your home, then look for substitutions that provide the same effect yet fit the space you have available. For example, if you want the look of a kentia palm but can't handle the 10-foot fronds, how about an areca palm that has the same form but only 3-foot fronds? An 8-foot-tall weeping fig is a beautiful plant, but you can select a 3-foot-tall specimen and place it on a pedestal to achieve a similar look. And you won't have to work around the 6-foot canopy spread.

Also, think about your decorating scheme. Although there are many reasons for acquiring a houseplant, one of the best is to complement a home's decor. Some plants seem to go hand in glove with a particular style of decorating, such as a cactus among southwestern-style furnishings.

You can also complement the features of a room through houseplant shape, size, and

To maintain the intense color of croton, place it in a window providing bright light. The result: a beauty to behold.

SUCCESS WITH HOUSEPLANTS
continued

Bamboo palms come in tiny pots when young; however, they grow to be sizable plants. Knowing this will help you successfully blend them into your decorating scheme.

color. Towering palms can be a powerful accent in the archway of an older home with high ceilings. A girl's room might call for a fluffy fern as a complement while a spiky dracaena could contrast with and tone down a country style. An all-white color scheme could use either a white African violet to emphasize and repeat the theme or a scarlet hibiscus as a contrasting focal point. By taking into account these factors, your new houseplant will provide a real statement about you and your house.

HEALTHY AND HEARTY: There are numerous sources for houseplants, each with its own pros and cons when it comes to bringing home healthy plants. Mail-order tropical-plant nurseries are among the best places to find rare and unusual houseplants. But the condition the plants arrive in depends as much on the vagaries of shipping as on the quality of the nursery. Be prepared for the occasional disappointment.

Local greenhouses often carry a variety of unusual plants as well as the old reliables. However, because these plants grow in nearly ideal conditions, they often have the most trouble adjusting to your home.

Garden centers, grocery stores, and building supply stores are fast becoming the "hot" sources for houseplants. Not only do they sell easy-care indoor plants at reasonable prices, but their offerings broaden in variety each year. Usually, plants from these sources have been through a lot during shipping. For that reason, they often thrive when you take them home to your slightly better conditions. On the other hand, they may bring along spider mites and diseases. Inspect plants carefully before purchasing to ensure their good health.

Many of us have a soft spot when it comes to sickly plants that the store is about to toss out. Resist the urge to buy such "bargains." Plants on their last legs rarely get any better. They also can introduce insects or diseases to the other plants at home.

Familiarizing yourself with the kinds of problems you might run into can keep you out of trouble. The information on page 44 will help you there.

If you discover a plant with damaged leaves, take a closer look; you might find the critter responsible, like the scale insects above. Resist the urge to take home damaged plants—you will only introduce insects to your other plants.

WELCOME HOME

After you get the plant home, check it for pests you might have missed. It's easy to say that there are only a few aphids and that you can take care of them quickly. But all it takes is for one to escape, and they will soon be all over your other plants.

Some gardeners routinely spray new plants with insecticidal soap, but if you've checked the plants thoroughly, you shouldn't have to take this step. Besides, a plant being moved from a greenhouse to your home will already suffer a slight bit of stress from the move, and spraying it with anything will only compound its problems.

Although your first inclination after bringing a plant home is to place it where you can enjoy it, it's better to take time to let it acclimate to its new spot. Remember, the conditions in your home most likely are different than those in the store. If you can bear to do so, isolate the plant from your other plants just in case you missed a pest problem. Use this isolation time to give the plant a few days in the best light possible. Then move it to the site you have selected.

Taking this time to acclimate your new plant will pay off in a plant that adjusts better and will not have problems such as leaf loss. And if a pest problem does show up while the plant is isolated, you don't have to panic. As long as you catch the problem early, it should be relatively easy to take care of it using the Integrated Pest Management (IPM) principles described on page 45. Keep the plant isolated until you are sure that you have taken care of the problem.

THE LONG HAUL

Once you have your plants in place at home, settle in to regular care. You can set up a schedule that's complicated or one that's simple. You can keep elaborate notes about how and when you watered, fertilized, repotted, and so forth. Or, you can merely set aside time on Saturday morning to look at your plants and determine what they need. You will not always be able to get all your watering done in one day because most likely the plants will have different requirements. But you can at least check them and make a mental note that you need to water the gloxinia on Tuesday, or that the peace lily doesn't need water again this week.

Grouping a collection of houseplants provides an attractive method of display, especially when the plants are healthy and thriving.

A giant euphorbia, the focal point in this room, naturally complements the southwestern decor. Using plants to enhance your decor—taking into account color, shape, and texture—makes your decorating scheme even more successful.

QUESTIONS?

Once your new plants have settled in to the perfect spot in their new home and you adjust to their requirements, you will undoubtedly discover a need for more information on care. Plants have their nuances just like people, and every once in a while you will come up against a "behavior" you can't figure out.

That's where we come in. In the pages that follow, you will find tips and advice on caring for plants, from choosing a pot and a spot to grow a plant to information about watering and fertilizing. If you are unable to figure out a problem, we will give you the tools you need to diagnose and fix it. Be aware that sometimes the best fix for a problem is to throw the plant away.

Last of all, we offer you a splendid pictorial look at our pick of the best, easiest-to-care-for houseplants. The "Directory of Houseplants," beginning on page 58, is filled with information on individual plants. You can browse through it to choose a new plant, to identify a plant you already have, or merely to gain a little more specific information about one of your plants. The directory provides each plant's cultural needs, methods for propagating it, information on pests to watch for, and other growing tips.

VALUE OF PLANTS: MENTAL AND PHYSICAL HEALTH

Research shows that plants ease everyday stress. In fact, students often do better on tests with plants in the room. These children taking a spelling test will be under less pressure than kids in a typical classroom.

Plants make us happy. The soft greens add beauty to our lives, and the smell and feel of greenery help soften some of the harsh elements in our everyday routines.

Research shows that working with and handling plants lowers blood pressure, eases stress, and generally makes us feel better. Growing plants, whether vegetables for the table or flowers for their beauty, appeals to almost everyone, and can bring a moment of peace or a few minutes of joy to an otherwise cheerless life. Indoor plants provide a chance to interact with nature. They give us pleasure in return for caring for them, which is a basic emotional need of humans.

Members of the American Horticultural Therapy Association (AHTA) use plant growing as a fundamental part of their therapy plans.

They develop horticulture programs for the elderly and disabled in nursing homes and for surgery and chemotherapy patients in hospitals. They also form gardening plans for the residents of group homes and prisons.

The AHTA philosophy relies on the fact that plants appeal to everyone's senses, even when those senses are somewhat diminished. The use of richly or brightly colored plants can be exciting or soothing to the eyes. The smells of foliage, soil, moisture, and fragrant flowers can make us feel peaceful and serene or even evoke pleasant memories. AHTA members also make frequent use of textural plants in their therapy. Touching plants calms us, whether it is performing the tasks of softly wiping leaves, pinching out the tips of a wayward vine, or merely stroking the soft, fuzzy leaves of a panda plant.

In the medical field, exposure to plants has been shown to help in many ways. It can minimize the time spent in a hospital after surgery, as well as reduce the amount and potency of painkillers requested by the patients. In a study at the Sloan-Kettering Institute, breast cancer surgery patients gathered their strength faster, increased their ability to focus attention, and reduced their depression by taking walks regularly in a garden.

These positive effects are evident in the business world as well. In an article in the *Journal of the Mississippi Academy of Sciences* in 1996, it was shown that plants not only raise humidity levels, making the workplace more comfortable, but the moisture they give to the air seems to suppress airborne microbes. In a study by Washington State University, people with plants in their work environment were 12 percent more productive and had lower blood pressure than those without. Need we say more about the positive aspects of adding plants to all aspects of our everyday lives?

A patient who's surrounded by plants recovers faster and tolerates a hospital stay with more ease. In extended care facilities, plants not only keep residents busy but also help them stay healthy.

Everyone deserves a tranquil retreat, a place to let go of the pressures of the day. Filling this sanctuary with plants will help you relax and allow stress to slip away.

INDOOR AIR POLLUTION

In our world of energy-efficient houses and office buildings sealed against the elements, it is alarming to find the number of pollutants that are our constant roommates. Copy machines and printers, rug pads, insulation and other synthetic materials, veneer furniture, products made of pressed wood and plywood, smoke, and detergents all give off pollutants, such as benzene, trichloroethylene, xylene, ammonia and formaldehyde. Studies by the EPA indicate that indoor air pollution is one of the fastest growing environmental problems.

How can we reduce these troubling substances in our lives? Plants reduce indoor pollution and thus provide us with a healthier physical atmosphere. They absorb pollutants through their leaves, where naturally occurring microorganisms break down the chemicals. Some absorption and breakdown also occurs in potting soil.

The original research on plant filtering began with NASA, where the need to find ways to reduce the high amount of pollutants emitted by equipment on the space shuttle was discovered. Researchers at the National Space Technology Lab found that houseplants reduced pollutants, particularly nitrogen and formaldehyde. In fact, just a single spider plant in an enclosed chamber filled with formaldehyde removed 85 percent of the pollutant in a day. As few as 15 plants can significantly reduce pollutants in the average house. The study suggested that we use one potted plant for every 100 square feet of floor space for pollution control.

Besides controlling gaseous pollution in the home, plant leaves clean air by trapping particulate matter. And, in their natural process of respiration, plants absorb our waste product—carbon dioxide—and furnish us oxygen and moisture. The old myth about avoiding plants in the bedroom because they use up air couldn't be further from the truth.

Spider plants, popular because they are so easy to care for, are great accessories for your home because of their amazing ability to absorb indoor pollutants. NASA uses them on the space shuttle to absorb formaldehyde.

An unassuming philodendron sitting in a corner quietly absorbs and renders inert the pollutants that are often so abundant in our homes.

BEST ABSORBERS

BAMBOO PALM
Formaldehyde
DRACAENA
Benzene
Formaldehyde
Trichloroethylene
ENGLISH IVY
Benzene
GOLDEN POTHOS
Formaldehyde
PHILODENDRON
Formaldehyde
SANSEVIERIA
Formaldehyde
SPATHIPHYLLUM
Benzene
Trichloroethylene
SPIDER PLANT
Formaldehyde

COMMON SOURCES OF INDOOR AIR POLLUTION

FORMALDEHYDE: Carpeting, pressed wood, fiberboard, foam insulation, paper products
HYDROCARBONS: Vinyl furniture, detergents, fabric softener
NITROGEN DIOXIDE: Malfunctioning furnaces, water heaters, leaking chimneys
BENZENE: Glue, spot remover, paint, varnish, paint stripper
METHYLENE CHLORIDE: Paint stripper, aerosols
TRICHLOROETHYLENE: Ink, paint, lacquer, varnish, adhesive

RIGHT PLANT
IN THE RIGHT PLACE

Schlumbergia species are native to Brazil. For that reason, to initiate flower buds, Christmas cactus needs to be in a spot where the temperature drops in fall and nights last at least 12 hours. Once buds form, the plant can be moved to a window.

An indoor waterfall creates a humid atmosphere. Plants native to the rain forest will take advantage of the moisture and thrive here.

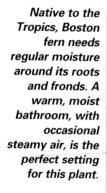 

Native to the Tropics, Boston fern needs regular moisture around its roots and fronds. A warm, moist bathroom, with occasional steamy air, is the perfect setting for this plant.

In order to pick the right spot in your home for a plant to thrive, it will help to understand the plant's origin and the conditions under which it grows in the wild. Luckily, most plants from tropical or desert areas are well adapted for life indoors. In most cases, either the conditions in our homes and offices match what the plant needs or the plant is able to adapt.

HOUSEPLANT ORIGINS

THE TROPICS: In the Tropics, temperatures remain constant, never dropping below freezing or rising above the mid-80s. On the rain forest floor, temperatures are cooler than high in the forest canopy; light ranges from moderate to low and moisture is abundant. Plants growing there tend to have large, dark-green leaves to take advantage of whatever light they get. Because there is little wind on the rain forest floor, the leaves have not developed adaptations to withstand tattering and instead are thin and delicate.

Rain forest plants that live high in the trees as epiphytes are accustomed to warm temperatures and fairly abundant light. They have minimal root systems and must be given plenty of moisture and humidity. Their leaves are thick and leathery to enable the plant to conserve moisture. And the leaves often form a vase to collect water.

MONSOONAL REGIONS: Plants from summer monsoon and hurricane areas are used to constantly warm temperatures and high humidity. Those from the southeastern United States will also tolerate a wide range of temperatures. Plants growing in high humidity tend to have thin leaves with little capacity to store water. In monsoonal regions, they have also evolved strong leaves and root systems to withstand wind.

MEDITERRANEAN AND SAVANNA CLIMATES: Plants of the Mediterranean region and African savanna thrive during hot days, cool nights, infrequent rainfall, and low humidity. They are much more adaptable to temperature changes than rain forest plants, although high humidity can stress them.

Crown-of-thorns, from dry, windy regions, has small leaves to conserve moisture.

Most plants from this region have small, leathery gray-green leaves, which are well adapted to conserving moisture. The leaves have a reduced leaf surface from which water can transpire. Many plants are also extremely aromatic because their pungent oils are made stronger by lack of moisture. Most herbs come from these regions.

Wax plants, native to dry regions, have waxy leaves to retain precious moisture.

Cacti have no leaves, only spines and thick stems, both of which keep in precious moisture.

Bulbous roots are another adaptation to conserve water. These roots also help plants survive the fires that sweep through savannas. Other plants have evolved hairy leaf surfaces to reduce moisture loss or very light colors to reflect the intense light and thus reduce the heat that enters the tissues.

DESERTS: Plants from arid or semi-arid deserts are accustomed to fluctuating moisture. Many have mechanisms for storing their own water, and because of this adaptability they make great houseplants. Plants of desert regions almost always have specialized methods or structures for dealing with aridity.

Cacti, in particular, have leaves that are reduced to spines with few stomates (openings) and a waxy covering to cut water loss. Their succulent, swollen tissues store water, helping the plants tolerate long periods of dryness. Grown as houseplants, cacti generally need well-drained sandy soil, infrequent watering to mimic the rain patterns in the desert, little to no fertilization, and high light for growth. They can usually tolerate lower light levels during their dormant period.

Plants from areas with hot summers, cold winters, low humidity, and little rainfall are perhaps the best adapted to all types of microclimates. Although their light requirements vary, most of these plants can tolerate different amounts of light, as well as

Panda plants are covered in soft hairs to avoid water loss.

A typical home is fairly dry, so choose plants to take advantage of this or take steps to increase your humidity levels.

temperatures and humidity levels that vary.

TEMPERATE ZONE: We seldom see plants from temperate regions used as houseplants. Bonsai are the exceptions, but even they don't make good houseplants. Temperate plants need a full dormancy, induced by very cold temperatures. They are a challenge to grow and, although some gardeners like to try, it's hard to get temperatures low enough. Besides, true dormancy means that a deciduous plant will drop its leaves. Most of us don't want a plant that doesn't have leaves for several months a year. The dormancy experienced by tropical plants is merely a matter of slowed growth and reduced bloom rather than leaf loss. This quality is more tolerable in a houseplant.

REGIONAL PLANTS

TROPICS
Lipstick plant
MONSOON
Fatsia
MEDITERRANEAN
Baby's tears
DESERT
Cactus
TEMPERATE
English ivy

LIGHT

Light is the most critical element when choosing a location for a plant. Plants need light for photosynthesis, which produces the food and energy necessary to keep them alive, as well as to form the hormones that induce flowering. If a plant has otherwise perfect conditions yet is in more or less light than required for optimum growth, it will be stressed. And a stressed plant is an invitation to trouble.

Light is much more than the amount of sun entering a window during the day. Plants are affected by the amount of light (its intensity), the color of light (its quality), and how long it lasts (its duration).

ALL ABOUT LIGHT

INTENSITY: The amount of light available—intensity—is often measured in foot-candles. Unfortunately, our eyes don't accurately sense levels of light because our pupils automatically adjust to the light around us. The only way to really measure the intensity is with a light meter.

If you don't want to be bothered with finding a meter and keeping accurate measurements, use your best reasoning about the amount of light shining in a window. The following guidelines will help you assess the amount of light a room receives. Or, you can try growing plants in one location for several weeks and then move them around to see how well they perform.

Depending on location and time of year, east and west windows receive a few hours of direct sun each day, with the west sun being hotter. South windows can receive five, six, or more hours of direct sun in winter and sometimes only indirect light in summer. North windows never receive direct light, and the amount of indirect light received depends on reflective surfaces nearby.

However, other factors can affect how much light a room actually receives. For example, as the seasons change, so does the angle of the sun hitting a window. So, more or less light will enter a room over the course of a year. Also, outdoor elements, such as awnings, neighboring buildings, and trees, can reduce light coming in, while reflective surfaces (indoors and out) can increase it.

The amount of light a plant receives varies widely depending on its distance from the primary light source. For instance, a much greater amount of light will fall on a plant if placed 6 inches from a window rather than at 2 feet from the same window. For that reason, a plant that requires moderate light will do well snuggled up to an east window or placed a few feet away from a west window.

QUALITY: Light can come from several sources. The most important is the sun. Direct sunlight has the greatest range of colors from the spectrum and the greatest intensity, compared to artificial light. Reflected light, whether off a building outdoors or off a white wall or mirror inside, can add to the light in a room. However, the quality of the light is much reduced from that of direct light, so you may still need to add supplemental lighting.

DURATION: The length of time that houseplants receive light is important because plants need a certain ratio between light and dark periods. Most require 8 to 16 hours of light every day. The cycle of light and dark and the length of each period is particularly critical for blooming plants because it helps trigger flower production. Plants given too many hours of light each day tend to have elongated or curled leaves, and eventually leaf loss. Too few hours of light causes stretching and very thin, easily damaged leaves. You can control this ratio by adding supplemental light to lengthen the day or covering the plants to give more hours of darkness. In fact, you can force many houseplants to bloom by altering these factors.

These windows at different angles show light variations. The right window has the brightest light; the left window has filtered light due to the angle and the stained glass panel.

The closer to the window, the more intense the light, the longer the light lasts and the broader the light's color spectrum.

Summer

Winter

Sunlight at a window will change depending on the season. In a south window in winter, sunlight will be less intense but will last longer.

PUTTING IT ALL TOGETHER

You will need to consider your specific conditions when deciding whether you have the right amount of light. For example, if you have a west window in which to grow a plant needing high light but there is a building that blocks the west sun after only an hour, you have the intensity but not the duration that you need.

If your south windows are shaded in summer by deciduous trees, your light intensity will be reduced, so your high-light plants that thrive in that window in winter may languish in summer.

If you have a north window that looks out on a tall, white building, you will have a considerable amount of reflected light. Reflected light is not of sufficient quality to grow a high-light plant, but you may be able to grow a medium-light plant in that window.

As you can see, all three elements—intensity, quality, and duration—must be considered. Although this may all seem confusing, the important thing to remember is to keep yourself constantly aware in order to note changes in your plant's health.

PLANTS' LIGHT NEEDS

Generally, plants are categorized as low-, medium-, or high-light plants. These categories list the optimum conditions, although some plants will thrive in a variety of light levels. Plants may do fine with slightly more or less light than is optimal. However, drastically different amounts of light will often cause a plant to languish. They may be damaged from too much light or direct sun, or they may stretch and become spindly with too little light.

Levels of light needed for plants to grow, as opposed to merely survive, may vary widely. Lower light may be sufficient to maintain a plant and keep it looking good, but not enough to get it to bloom.

A FEW GUIDELINES ABOUT LIGHT

■ High light usually refers to a southern or western exposure.
■ Medium light usually means a western or eastern exposure. Plants receive a few hours of sun each day, morning sun in an east window and late afternoon sun in a west window.
■ Low light usually refers to an eastern or northern exposure or to a room's interior.
■ A sheer curtain lessens the light intensity and heat in a south or west window, making the situation appropriate for a medium-light plant.
■ Flowering plants usually need high light.
■ Low-light plants usually do well in east, northeast or north windows, where they get mostly indirect light.
■ The intensity of direct light varies according to the season. When the sun is higher in the sky in summer in the northern hemisphere, the light is more intense and hotter, but the duration of light is less because the sun is higher. In winter the sun is lower in the sky, with a longer duration of light but with less intensity.
■ A south window has much more direct light in winter than in summer. It is also hotter in summer.
■ A west window is usually hotter than a south window because of the concentrated quality of the sunlight in the late afternoon.

SUPPLEMENTAL LIGHT

If you don't have the right amount of light for what you want to grow, it's possible to enhance the natural light with artificial lighting. There are two basic ways to do this. One, supplement the natural light by either combining lights with daylight or using them to provide a longer day. And two, you can grow plants entirely with artificial light.

Good supplemental light sources provide more light than heat. Plants respond best to the full spectrum of sunlight, and there are several options for getting a wide spectrum.

A light cart or light garden can be simply utilitarian or serve as an attractive feature of the room's decor.

TYPES OF LIGHTS

INCANDESCENTS: The bulbs found in lamps and room fixtures, incandescent lights, are usually not appropriate for supplemental lighting. They're hot and emit only the red-orange part of the spectrum, which is too narrow for plants to thrive.

FLUORESCENTS: Fluorescent lights remain cool, allowing plants to grow much closer to the tubes without damage. They also cost less and use less electricity than other lights.

There are three types of fluorescent lights. Warm-white tubes have an enhanced red range, and cool whites have an enhanced blue range. A combination provides a wide, although not full, spectrum.

The third fluorescent type is often referred to as a grow light. Emitting almost 90 percent of the sun's spectrum, grow lights cost more than standard fluorescent bulbs but fit in standard fixtures.

To be effective, fluorescents must be close to the plants. A plant whose canopy is 6 inches below a fixture with two 40-watt tubes and a reflector will receive 900 foot-candles of light, about the same as in an east window in summer. This intensity drops by half for each additional 6 inches from the tubes.

For a broad color spectrum, you can combine fluorescent tubes with incandescent bulbs. The combination makes the room and the people in it look better than with fluorescent-only lighting. You must carefully arrange the room, though, because the plants must be close to the fluorescent fixture yet far enough away from the incandescent light to avoid damage.

HIGH-INTENSITY LAMPS: By far the most efficient supplemental lighting, high-intensity lamps work best in large areas. They are more expensive than fluorescent lights but are worth it if you need a great deal of supplemental lighting. There are several types:

■ METAL HALIDE: With the best spectrum for the largest number of plants, halide lamps are intense enough to work in areas with limited or no natural light. They can even be used to grow vegetables and fruit. Metal halide lamps give off about 20 percent more light than fluorescent lights and range in wattage from 175 to 1500. For a typical home indoor garden in a living area, 400 watts is adequate.

■ HIGH-PRESSURE SODIUM: The enhanced red-orange color range of these is best for flowering plants. Use them as a supplement to natural light. They give off an amber glow, which may distort colors in your home.

■ LOW-PRESSURE SODIUM: Low-pressure sodium lamps and mercury discharge lamps are generally only used commercially.

If you are serious about indoor lighting, use a combination of high-intensity halide and sodium lamps. High-intensity lights come in all wattages. In order to figure out what you need, use the following guidelines:

As the sole lighting source, 400 watts effectively lights 25 square feet. As a supplement, 400 watts will cover 64 square feet, and 1,000 watts will effectively light 144 square feet. For smaller areas, use lower wattage bulbs.

All types of lights lose effectiveness over time, so replace bulbs regularly, especially fluorescent tubes. Follow the manufacturer's recommendations for replacement, but as a general rule, switch bulbs after a year of use. Also, be sure the fixtures have a white reflector to make the best use of the light.

Supplemental light fixtures are fairly basic. The main differences are in the bulbs. Choose supplemental lighting according to your plants' needs and your budget.

PUTTING TOGETHER A LIGHT GARDEN

Looking for inexpensive supplemental lighting? Build the light stand at left for around $75.

The stand holds a standard greenhouse flat and fits on a tabletop. It also uses a standard, 2-foot two-tube fluorescent fixture. Raising and lowering the light is easy because the fixture is attached to the legs of the stand by carriage bolts and wing nuts. The legs are made of heavy lumber for stability, and if you need to transport the stand, they come off. One of the details that makes this project particularly simple for novice do-it-yourselfers is that there are no miter joints, only butt joints.

Using a handsaw or power trim saw, cut the 1×3s straight across into four 2-foot-long pieces. These are the legs. Drill pairs of holes every 4 inches down the legs, starting 1½ inches from the top. Each pair should be 2 inches apart. Use a carpenters square to ensure each hole is exactly opposite the other hole and level with the holes on the other legs.

Next, cut the 1×4 into two 2-foot-long sections and two 1-foot sections. The 2-foot pieces form the sides of the light box; the 1-foot sections are the ends. Glue the pieces together to form the box, reinforcing the joints with brads. Cut four 1-foot-long strips from the remaining 1×3. Glue and tack the strips across the top of the box as reinforcement and to hang the light fixture from.

Drill holes in the end of the light box to correspond with the holes in the legs. Attach the legs to the light box with carriage bolts and wing nuts. Finally, attach the light unit to the light box following manufacturer's directions.

To dress up the light stand, glue and nail decorative molding to the legs and light box. Molding is available in many patterns, some plain and others with carved designs, as in the examples here. You can stain the molding, paint it, or let it naturally age.

MATERIALS LIST

8 feet – 1×4
16 feet – 1×3
8 feet – 2¼-inch molding
8 feet – 4¼-inch molding
16 – 1¾ × ¼-inch bolts, wing nuts, washers
1 – 12-foot electrical cord
1 – 24-inch two-bulb fluorescent light unit
1½-inch brads
Waterproof wood glue

Plant pigment—chlorophyll—absorbs light mainly in the violet, blue, and red wavelengths. Green light is reflected, giving plants their green appearance. Sunlight contains all wavelengths.

Plants under lights need 8 to 16 hours of lighting every day. Using a timer ensures the right amount. After setting the timer, watch your plants for the next few weeks and adjust the cycle as needed. Also, adjust it as the sun's intensity and duration changes over the year. If using fluorescents, rotate plants regularly; the ends of the bulbs don't provide as intense a light as the centers. Or, put low-light plants toward the ends and high-light plants in the center.

INDOOR LIGHTING COSTS

Light	Fixture Cost (includes reflector, ballast)	Bulb Cost	Amount of Light (in lumens)	Life span (in hours)
HALIDE				
250 watt	$180–$300	$45	23,000	10,000
400 watt	$180–$300	$45	40,000	20,000
1000 watt	$180–$300	$75	115,000	12,000
SODIUM				
250 watt	$240–$350	$30	27,500	24,000
400 watt	$240–$350	$30	50,000	24,000
1000 watt	$240–$350	$80	140,000	24,000
FLUORESCENT				
40 watt, cool	$15–$30 Ballast replacement cost: $3–$40 (depends on quality)	$6-8 for 2	2,250–3,200	20,000
40 watt, warm	$15–$30 Ballast replacement cost: $3–$40 (depends on quality)	$6-8 for 2	1,880–3,200	20,000
40 watt, full spectrum	$15–$30 Ballast replacement cost: $3–$40 (depends on quality)	$6-8 for 2	2,200	20,000
INCANDESCENT				
60 watt	$1–$20+ (depending on style)	$1.50–$2.50 for 4	870–900	1,000
75 watt	$1–$20+ (depending on style)	$1.50–$2.50 for 4	1,100–1,150	750–1,000
100 watt	$1–$20+ (depending on style)	$1.50–$2.50 for 4	1,700–1,800	750–1,000

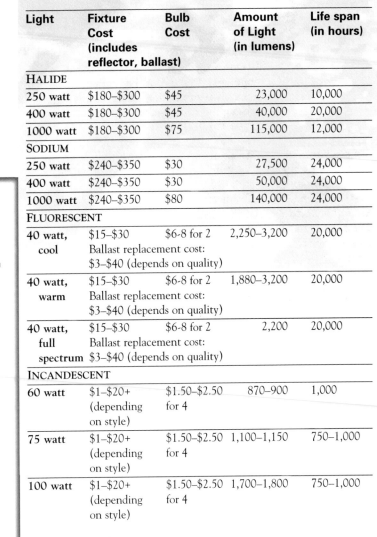

TEMPERATURE, HUMIDITY, AND AIR CIRCULATION

A ceiling fan helps move air around, creating a healthier atmosphere for your plants. Circulating air prohibits disease problems, which allows plants to become sturdier.

Most homes maintain a year-round temperature of 60° to 75° F. Happily, most houseplants are perfectly suited to these temperatures. If you can, try to give your plants at least a 5° F drop at night. Plants have evolved to take advantage of variations in day and night temperatures. In fact, a 10° F drop can trigger blooms in orchids, flowering maples, and other plants.

Even indoors, seasonal temperatures will vary somewhat. Put plants that need a cool, dormant period in your coolest spots. In your hottest areas, use plants that thrive on heat, such as cactus and euphorbia. There may be great variations within a single room that can be used to advantage once you are aware of them. They can also spell disaster if you're not. For example, cold drafts near windows and entrances in winter can make plants cold, in which case their leaves will droop. When the temperature drops below 50° F, drafts can injure plants through chilling. The injury shows up on the leaves, which appear water soaked or blackened.

Hot areas occur around fireplaces, heat vents, incandescent lights, and windows in summer. Also, areas with poor air circulation tend to be hotter. Plants that can't take the heat will become spindly and limp.

HUMIDITY

Humidity is the percentage of water in the air. As air warms, it holds more water, and so the humidity is higher. In winter, the cooler temperatures mean the humidity is naturally lower. Also, home heating systems dry out the air. Air conditioning reduces humidity as

well, so your plant's climate will change with the seasons. The humidity in the native habitat of tropical and subtropical plants runs about 80 percent, while most houses average between 35 to 65 percent humidity and sometimes fall below 20 percent in winter. Luckily, many plants can adapt to a lower humidity level.

When humidity is too low, plants exhibit a variety of symptoms, the most common being brown tips on the leaves. Low-humidity problems are intensified if soil is allowed to dry out, if the plant is in a draft, or if it is flooded with unfiltered sunlight. High humidity is seldom a problem except in rooms devoted to indoor pools and hot tubs.

For plants that require high humidity, it's possible to create a humid microclimate, that is, to raise the humidity in a small area. It takes quite a bit of work to maintain plants needing high humidity, though, so keep this in mind when making your selections.

To keep humidity high, you must not only put more water into the air but also reduce air circulation, which evaporates water from around the plant. Reducing air circulation

Plants grouped together will have higher humidity levels around each plant. If they are spread farther apart, air circulation will remove some of the humidity.

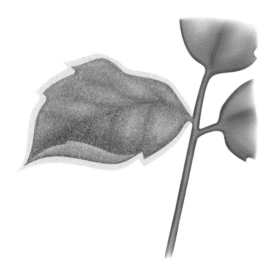

Plants continually release water vapor through openings in their leaves called stomates. This creates a moist layer of air surrounding the leaf surface, a boundary layer. Boundary layers are crucial to healthy plants. Too thick, and the plant is susceptible to fungal disease. Too thin—perhaps because wind blows it away—and the plant is subject to water stress.

can cause problems with fungal growth, so it's important to find a successful balance.

MANAGING HUMIDITY

There are several effective ways to manage humidity in a house. You can measure the specific humidity in a particular room, but this will vary widely around the house. It is usually effective to watch plants closely and adjust according to how they perform.

The most efficient way to raise humidity is to install a humidifier on your furnace. This theoretically lets you control the humidity throughout the house. Even with such a system, though, humidity levels may still vary.

Hand-misting or wetting foliage is a common recommendation for humidity-loving plants, but in reality this only temporarily puts moisture into the air. If the rest of the room is dry, that moisture will evaporate quickly. You would have to mist every few hours for this technique to be effective. Besides, wetting the leaves of many plants invites disease problems.

Grouping plants helps raise humidity by reducing the air circulation inside the group and keeping moisture levels higher than if air freely circulates around a single plant. Put the plants with the highest humidity needs in the center of the grouping and the more adaptable plants on the outer edges.

One fairly effective way to raise the humidity immediately surrounding a plant is to set its pot on a tray of pebbles covered with water. As long as there is water in the tray, it will evaporate into the air. If the room

surrounding the plant is extremely dry, this may not do much good. However, in average humidity, this method helps plants that need more moisture. When filling the gravel bed with water, make sure the water doesn't touch the bottom of the pot, where it can saturate the soil. You can also set the pots in their saucers on top of pebbles.

Double-potting a plant is another way to raise humidity around a plant. Fill the void between the pots with long-fibered sphagnum or Spanish moss, and dampen the moss. Remove the moss periodically to check the bottom of the pots for standing water.

AIR CIRCULATION

A companion element to humidity is air circulation. Air movement removes moisture from the leaves and therefore prevents disease. It also benefits plants in other ways. Regular movement of the leaves produces sturdier, denser plants. In addition, good air movement may keep some insect populations in check.

You can increase air movement by opening a window in warm weather, but only when the weather cooperates. Otherwise, a ceiling fan will keep the air moving, as will small fans placed near plants.

It all comes down to watching your plants carefully. Raise the humidity if plants show signs of drying out and increase the air circulation if you encounter insect or fungal problems. Your plants will let you know what suits them the best if you pay attention.

Mulching a plant slows evaporation from the soil, keeping soil moist for a longer time. This also keeps moisture in the air around the plant, raising humidity. Mulch also enhances the appearance of the plant.

YOUR HOME'S CONDITIONS

Every room has many different conditions that you can use to advantage for siting plants. Drafty doors and windows, heat registers, dark corners, and high, warm bookshelves all create special microclimates.

You know your home and its little idiosyncrasies better than anyone else. You are the perfect person to find the best location for your houseplants to thrive. Once you understand a plant's origin and under what conditions it grows in the wild, you can map out the areas in your home that are the most appropriate. And, you will be able to pick out just the right spot.

When choosing a location in your home, of course, you need to consider light, humidity, temperature, and air circulation. As a general guideline, immediately eliminate really hot, sunny areas or very dark spots. If you have any doubts about a spot's suitability for a particular plant, it's okay to experiment. Just be aware that your plant may not look its best or may not survive.

You must also recognize that microclimates will change with the season and the weather, so your plants may be in the perfect situation in winter and need to be sited elsewhere for the summer months.

HEAT AND HUMIDITY

The best temperature range for most plants is between 60° to 75° F. Even more critical is to make sure that you have a 5° to 10° F drop at night. Once you adjust your temperature, make note of the different microclimates in your house according to light intensity and humidity.

If you have a plant that requires cool temperatures, a sunny, unheated porch or spot close to a window in winter will give you a cool microclimate. Foyers and entryways can also provide cool temperatures, but not consistently. When the door is opened, there may be an influx of cool, even cold, air in winter. Then the area goes back to its original temperature. In summer, this same entryway or foyer will be filled with bursts of hot air, fine for a cactus but deadly to a sensitive, thin-leaved tropical plant.

In this situation, you must have a fairly tough plant. It must be tolerant of changes in temperature, as well as a good bit of air circulation and even drying drafts. Less-tolerant plants may be damaged.

Since hot air rises, the top shelf of a bookcase or the top of a kitchen cabinet can provide an extra bit of warmth for a plant that doesn't tolerate cold. These locations are also out of the way enough that the plant won't face much air movement. However, because they are more remote, you will need to be extra careful not to neglect them.

The tendency for hot air to rise means that the floor will be cooler, so this is a great place for plants that don't tolerate natural summer heat or home heating in winter.

Turning on the heat in the house for the winter naturally dries out the air, so be ready with your pebble trays or humidifiers to make up for lost moisture. If you are growing only arid plants, this is not an issue, but tropical plants suddenly deprived of moisture can suffer, sometimes drastically.

Keep plants away from drafts when the air conditioning is running. If you close the shades to keep the house cool in summer, you may need to give high-light plants some additional lighting. Put medium- and low-light plants in higher light when you can, and expect them to adjust by dropping leaves or elongating between nodes. Some plants, though, may respond to the lower light positively because the summer sun is so intense.

light intensity from south windows won't be quite as high as in winter.

North windows keep a room quite cool in winter, making this a perfect spot to place plants that need a cool, dormant period. The same north room in summer can be a cool spot for plants that don't withstand heat as long as you realize that the light intensity is much lower than in a room with a different orientation. Be ready with supplemental light if necessary.

Use areas directly next to windows to your advantage, but be careful not to set a plant too near cold glass in winter. All it takes is one really cold night to do permanent chilling damage to a cool-sensitive plant. However, plants that require a cool, dormant period during the winter are perfectly suited to a cold windowsill.

VENTS: Areas around heat registers and air conditioning vents have their own special problems. They produce high air turnover and dry things out. Plants native to arid climates can tolerate this dry air blowing over them, but many tropical plants cannot. If you need good air circulation to prevent fungal problems, you will be better off using a fan to move air than to set plants near vents and registers.

FIREPLACES: Likewise, a situation above a fireplace will have fluctuating dry, hot periods. Beware of putting a plant directly on a mantel, regardless of how good it looks. You may have a beautifully draped English ivy gracing your fireplace only to find it sizzled and crisp if you forget to move it before the first fire of the winter season.

BATHROOMS AND KITCHENS: Bathrooms and kitchens naturally have more humidity than the rest of the house. You can take advantage of this situation by putting plants in these rooms that are used to and need the almost constant humidity of the rain forest.

Another thing to keep in mind is that, unless you never use your kitchen, plants in this room will, over time, accumulate greasy dirt on the leaves. Figure extra time in your schedule to wash them regularly, using a dilute solution of dishwashing detergent.

As you move your plants around, be prepared for them to react to the change. They might drop their leaves or seem to react poorly. If you know their needs and care for them accordingly, they will come through the changes just fine.

PLANTS TO MATCH CONDITION

STEAMY BATHROOM
Flamingo flower
Cape primrose
Coleus
Croton
Ferns
Hibiscus

COOL FOYER
Cactus
Citrus
Japanese fatsia
Spider plant
Umbrella plant

COOL SUNROOM (IN WINTER)
Asparagus fern
Cactus
Christmas cactus
Clivia
English ivy
Artillary plant
Swedish ivy

WARM SUNROOM (IN SUMMER)
Bromeliads
Cactus
Crown-of-thorns
Grape ivy
Wax plant
Jade
Kalanchoes
Nerve plant
Ponytail palm

DARK CORNER IN COOL LIVING ROOM
Cast-iron plant
Chinese evergreen
Dracaenas
Fishtail palm
Lady palm
Snake plant
Philodendrons

HOME CLIMATES

WINDOWS: A room with an abundance of windows will have varying microclimates, depending on the season and time of day. South windows give a room extra warmth in winter, especially in the morning, since the angle of the sun is lower. In summer, the sun will be higher in the sky, and although a south-facing room may still be too warm for some plants, the

PLANTS HARMFUL TO KIDS AND PETS

Although most house-plants are perfectly harmless, the following may show some toxicity if ingested or if the sap gets on the skin:

Flamingo flower
Caladium
Clivia
Croton
Crown-of-thorns
Dumb cane
Pothos
Ficus
Fishtail palm
  (fruit only)
English ivy
Swiss cheese plant
Philodendron
Peace lily

DESIGNING WITH HOUSEPLANTS

This garden is full of energy—contrasting the tidy, rounded leaves of jade, the silvery puckered foliage of fittonia, the delicate look of baby's tears, and the elegant, wavy fronds of bird's-nest fern.

As beautiful as plants are in their own right, just having a collection of plants does not always produce the most pleasing indoor garden. However, by combining design principles, personal style, your home's decor, and the plants' natural aesthetic qualities, it is possible to create a stunning place to work or play.

If you keep in mind the plants' relationships to each other as you design, the sky's the limit as far as the looks you can achieve. Most importantly, don't be afraid to move things around in search of a better effect. Be willing to experiment.

DESIGN BASICS

As you begin to think about plant arrangement and choice, first decide what type of display you want to have. Do you want to display only plants in bloom, design a temporary arrangement that will change often, or focus on a permanent display? Do you want to feature a collection of plants or highlight only one? If displaying only one plant, the container becomes much more important than in groupings because it will be a focal point as well. Is this to be a collection of your favorite plants, or strictly a decorative addition to the room?

POINT OF VIEW

Once you've decided what type of display you want, determine the point or points from which it will be viewed. You may want to tuck your plants against a wall where you view them from only one or two sides. In this type of display, you will need something to serve as a backdrop. Also remember to leave room behind the display for air to circulate, as well as to allow access for routine watering and grooming.

The other type of view is an island grouping, designed to be appreciated from any direction. An island grouping needs a fairly large, open area that is accessible from all sides. This type of display will have increased air movement and varying light conditions.

FORMAL OR INFORMAL

Decide whether you want your indoor garden to have a formal or an informal appearance. Formal style tends to be symmetrical, with complementary shades of one color. There are no haphazard arrangements and no unruly spilling of foliage. Everything is neat and tight, such as the look you get with topiary plants or cacti.

Plant sizes are valuable elements in designing an indoor garden. Large plants have instant focus; small plants are intimate and subtle.

Informal style is asymmetrical and freely uses contrasting or complementary colors. There is more mixing of colors, wide use of textures and patterns, and loose, trailing plants, such as grape ivy and asparagus fern.

The next step is the most fun—selecting the plants. Take into consideration all of your environmental conditions. Then consider not only the individual plant characteristics but also the effect plants will have together and the ambience you want. Good combinations can make a run-of-the-mill collection of plants into a spectacular artistic display.

COMBINING PLANTS

Begin making a list of plants you want to use, considering the spaces you have available and each plant's mature size, texture, form, and color. Large plants make good "bones" of a display, much the same way shrubs and trees are used in the outdoor garden. Small plants create an intimate display and are effective ground covers in large pots. The most effective look comes from using varying heights, forms, and textures.

FORM: Plants come in a variety of shapes, from a vertical pothos (trained on a moss stake) or a spiky dracaena, to a horizontal Christmas cactus or sword fern. They may be softly mounded (polka-dot plant and peperomia), vase shaped (bromeliad), or trailing (Swedish ivy or philodendron). Dramatically different heights and shapes give your display excitement and keep the viewer constantly intrigued.

HEIGHT: Plant heights vary widely. Stair-stepping with shorter plants in front, medium in the center, and tall in back is traditional; however, sometimes breaking up this pattern produces an intriguing change. Keep plant sizes in mind as you start to design different combinations. A small plant, such as creeping fig, will be completely overpowered if placed next to a towering fiddleleaf fig.

You can make selections according to plant height, but it's also possible to vary this by "staging" or placing plants on inverted pots or pedestals to create different heights. This gives you the freedom to choose plants for their form and color.

TEXTURE: Although we tend to think of texture as the feel of a plant, it actually indicates the appearance rather than the actual physical feeling. Textures add movement, and you can use them to energize or calm any room. The large, smooth leaves of a peace lily calm and soothe, and the smaller, frisky leaves of a ming aralia spark energy. A combination of many types of leaf shapes and sizes offers your display attractive contrast and fills it with interest and diversity.

Combining sizes, shapes, and textures fills an indoor garden with life. Experiment and manipulate to satisfy your creative urges.

A grouping of similar-textured plants provides a display that is delightful in its simplicity.

A combination of a Madagascar dragontree with its spiky leaves, next to a Japanese fatsia or balfour aralia, with its billowing foliage, shows off the individual plants and also draws attention to their differences. Large, coarse textures will always be more obvious, so plant them farther from the viewer. Fine textures of small leaves tend to recede, so small leaves are most effective up close where the viewer can see them intimately.

COLOR: Picking colors is part of the fun of indoor gardening. Not only can you consider flowers of red, yellow, and blue, but you can also have a myriad of shades and hues of green to use in the plan. Foliage plants are particularly easy to design with because green is soothing to the eyes.

Bold colors are more difficult to use in a design but make beautiful statements as focal points. Consider what an impact bright scarlet hibiscus blossoms or rich red flamingo flower spathes will have. White and silver blend well with other colors and lighten plantings. For example, use silver-leaved peperomia or silver-variegated nerve plants as filler in a bright planting.

Plant shapes are as varied as people shapes. Add drama by contrasting vertical to horizontal, mounded to spiky, hanging to climbing.

DESIGN FOR YOUR HOME

Once you have an idea of the principles of design, you can apply them to your home. First, decide whether you intend to create a complete design for the entire house or individual plans for discrete areas. Next, consider these questions: Do you want the plants to be seen from the outside through a window or only from indoors? Will you see the display from a distant room, or will it be an intimate display seen from only one chair? Do you want to use a plant to hide something unattractive? What is your visual purpose? Do you want to add color to the room, to screen one room from another, to have plants around for enjoyment, to show off prized plants, or to break up an expanse of wall?

Ferns on pedestals repeat the symmetry of the windows flanking the door and mimic the botanical print of the bedspread.

Let personal style dictate your use of plants. For example, this ivy-filled bird cage fits well among other fanciful furnishings.

EVALUATE YOUR SPACE

You should take note of the different situations in your home: vaulted ceilings, a bay window with or without a window seat, a mantel framed by bookcases, a perfect window to function much as a picture frame for a specimen plant, or living areas that need to be screened by a type of divider. If you are designing for a conservatory, you will have an interesting situation with light from almost all sides. You may also have a situation with no light in which you will have to rely on artificial sources. You may even want to grow several display plants to rotate into a space with inadequate light for growing. Once one plant begins to look bad, replace it with one that has been growing in good light, and then transfer the inferior one into a better location for growing.

Also consider the color scheme of your room in the design process. Plants can be effective whether they are in colors contrasting or complementary to the room. As you choose containers, take care to highlight the plants as well as the room colors. Consider matching indoor and outdoor decor as well.

THE RIGHT PLACE

Think about where you want to place plants. If you don't have surfaces for them to occupy, consider installing hangers to display baskets of greenery. Try to keep plants off the tops of electrical equipment, such as televisions, stereos, and computers. As carefully as you may water, you still risk serious trouble with a spill. Also, keep plants out of the way of traffic to avoid damage to the plant and possible injury to a passerby. Especially, keep toxic plants out of the way of small children and pets.

Try to fit plants to the space you have. Logically, put a small plant in a small space and fill a large, open space with a large plant

A tall weeping fig and large-leaved palm serve as a backdrop for the sofa. They accent the large windows in this living area, as well as bring them into scale with the room.

A large plant, hanging ferns, spiky aloe, and baskets of colorful blooming plants enhance this room's country-casual feeling.

or with one that gives the impression of being large. If you have a great, open space, such as a room with a vaulted ceiling, you may not need a 10-foot palm to fill it. Instead, you can put a 5-foot palm on an attractive pedestal to give the illusion of a large plant.

YOUR OWN STYLE

Certain plants will evoke certain images, and you can use this to match or complement your room's decor. Southwestern decor creates a dry, almost sere feeling by using gray-green, peach, aqua, gold, and shades of brown. Cactus, crown-of-thorns, and Madagascar dragontree in pots with a sandy finish look like they belong in a Nevada desert.

In contrast, a Victorian garden is lush, feathery, and fussy, with lots of humidity. Colors that evoke this image are deep greens and blue-greens, and rich flower colors.

Palms, flowering maples, and ferns in fancy glazed pots, elaborate jardinieres, and natural-looking willow baskets fit beautifully into a Victorian room .

A contemporary garden is very architectural, with simple, sleek lines. Colors are bold, usually white, black, and red. Architectural plants, such as dracaena, kentia palm, or a solitary orchid, complement a contemporary scheme, particularly when placed in containers of bold colors, with simple, straight lines, and no ornamentation.

Oriental decor is similar to contemporary, with a great deal of attention paid to simple, bold lines. Colors are often muted with deep greens and grays and an occasional red accent. Palms and orchids are very popular, particularly when they are placed in bonsai-type pots of muted colors.

If you have doubts about choosing containers to match your decor, neutral-color pots will not take attention away from the plants. You can use the same type of pot throughout a grouping or vary them. You must figure out some way to connect them or you will end up with a jumble that is not appealing. You might use all terra-cotta pots with varied shapes. Or, you could use all glazed, straight-sided containers in different colors or even a grouping of different sizes of willow baskets.

Use the color of plants—that of the flowers and the foliage—to complement the furniture and accessories in a room.

Plants accent the architecture of a home. For example, this weeping fig graces corner windows in an alcove of a breakfast area.

SPECIAL EFFECTS

There are countless special effects you can create with plants to give your home or room a personal touch that no one else can duplicate. When you indulge in particular types of indoor plantings, such as the ones suggested here, your personality shines through in ways that more conventional designs rarely permit.

Plants can sometimes substitute for draperies. This one becomes a botanical picture frame, adding privacy without blocking light.

Orange blossoms will take your breath away with their intoxicating scent. The striking green and orange fruit add to the ambience of the indoor garden.

FLOWERING PLANTS

Although it may take a little more time for care, it is possible to have an indoor garden of strictly flowering plants. You will need to plan this garden carefully, since most flowering plants need plenty of light. Consider adding supplemental light to create that perfect setting. A garden of flowering maple, sweet olive, hibiscus, begonia, Christmas cactus, clivia, and African violet would make even a florist envious. Carefully planned, an all-flower garden can provide blooming plants year-round.

You are fortunate if you have the perfect conditions to grow flowering plants. However, the growing locations for the plants may differ from where you wanted to display them. Grow them there anyway, and when they reach their peak, move them. For example, rotate them onto the dining room table or into a prime spot on the mantel. When they finish blooming, move them back and replace them with something else that is blooming.

You can create a blooming curtain by placing a trellis in a window. Set pots of flowering vines on the windowsill and train them upward. Besides beautiful blossoms, the trellis serves to shade a room or act as a privacy screen. There are several traditional vines that work well, such as bougainvillea, passionflower, and jasmine. Also consider using nontraditional plants, such as morning glories, sweet peas, and scarlet runner beans. To attempt a variation on this theme, fasten a trellis against a wall or window, and then position small pots of flowering plants all over it.

It takes extra work to keep an indoor garden in continual bloom, but it can be done. Flowering kalanchoe adds a remarkable shock of orange or red color and blooms for an extended period.

ANNUAL PLANTS

You may think of annuals, such as impatiens, coleus, and geraniums, as belonging outdoors. Perhaps you've grown them on the windowsill for a spot of winter color and quickly put them outdoors in spring because they end up looking so bad. Annuals can be grown year-round indoors, and they can be beautiful. Geraniums and impatiens do especially well, as long as they have plenty of light and a cool spot. You will get the best results if you take cuttings of your outdoor plants in the fall and root them in individual pots. As they begin to grow, pinch them back to keep them bushy and small, and fertilize them every two weeks with a dilute solution. Remove faded flowers regularly to help keep them blooming.

FRUITING PLANTS

An offshoot of flowering plants is fruit-producing plants. Some of these, such as coralberry and coffee, are quite ornamental. You will usually have to hand-pollinate them for fruit to develop. Many will have flowers, green fruit, and ripe fruit on them at the same time, which makes

Harvest your own coffee beans. With its creamy white blossoms and green, red, and then brown berries, a coffee plant provides a beautiful addition to the blooming garden.

You don't need a fancy headboard when you have plants. Attach brackets and a shelf to the wall at the head of your bed, then set plants, here pothos, and accessories on the shelf.

for quite a show. Other popular fruiting plants are lemon, orange, and calamondin orange.

FUN PLANTS

What better way to amuse your friends or decorate a child's room than with funky plants. All it takes is a little imagination. Then have some fun.

Hang a string-of-beads or burro's tail from the ceiling in a beach pail or Easter basket. Grow scarlet runner beans in the window and then eat them. Fill an old fish tank with carnivorous plants, such as Venus flytrap and sundew. Raid the refrigerator and grow a pineapple by slicing off the top and planting it. Save orange or lemon seeds and start a citrus tree. Start an avocado or a sweet potato vine in water. Sweet potato vine can also be wound around a window to frame it, just like you would a picture.

Don't forget to add plants with unusual textures, such as panda plant and purple passion plant. Both of these plants are fuzzy enough to cuddle.

SPECIALTY GARDENS

There are countless types of specialty gardens to set up in your home, each with its own requirements. For example, a terrarium, dish garden, or a garden of cacti and succulents will give you a fairly care-free, contained garden. Another example of a garden that takes little time except for watering is one with all epiphytes. Some gardeners actually set up an epiphyte "tree" on which to grow the plants. You can grow an aquatic garden indoors as long as you choose plants that will tolerate low light and choose your containers carefully. Bonsai and orchid collections make beautiful, fairly formal home displays. Another type of formal planting is to use only standards or topiaries. Herbs and annual flowers do well when grown this way.

You can even grow edible plants, such as herbs and vegetables. Herbs do particularly well on a windowsill, and the only extra work you'll have is to prune them regularly to add to your cooking. Vegetables such as cherry tomatoes, small peppers, and lettuce will do well if you have plenty of light and are willing to hand-pollinate them to get fruit. If you don't have the light you need, but would still like to try this, a vegetable and herb garden makes a good introduction into the use of supplemental light.

Besides flower-producing plants, those that are fruit-producing, such as this lime, serve as showy specimens for your home. You may have to hand-pollinate to get them to fruit.

When choosing plants for a child's room, use your imagination. This wooden train becomes a perfect vehicle for showing off (from left) tall, spiky dracaena; gold-dust plant (another type of dracaena), variegated croton, and a small container of polka-dot plant.

GROWING THE BEST PLANTS

To bottom water, set the plant in a pan of water. Capillary action wicks the water through the soil to the plant roots. After half an hour, empty the saucer.

A plant's water requirements vary as the seasons change. Going by a set schedule doesn't take into account these variations, so instead you must keep an eye on houseplants. Take a look at all the factors that come into play.

■ Plants take up more water when humidity is low. If your skin is dry, plants are probably feeling desiccated, too. However, be aware that in the cooler, shorter days of winter, plant growth slows, a sign that they're using less water. So if you compensate for dry air by watering on a schedule suited to the warm days of summer, you may end up overwatering.

■ On the other side of the coin, high humidity slows transpiration, which reduces moisture uptake by roots. Unless the plant is in a breezy area, where wind moves moisture away from leaves, you'll need to water less often.

■ Overcast skies in spring and fall slow plant growth and reduce water requirements.

■ Plants in high light use more water than those in low light, depending on humidity.

If the soil has completely dried out, submerge the entire pot in a pan of tepid water for half an hour, then drain.

WHEN TO WATER

So, how do you know when to water? Simple. Give plants water when they need it. The secret lies in learning to recognize the individual signals each plant gives.

Look at your plant. A well-watered plant looks "right." Its tissues are firm because all the cells are filled with water; its leaves are glossy. Many plants flag before wilting, with leaves appearing slightly limp, losing their sheen and becoming pale. Flagging is a sure sign a plant needs water. If you catch a plant at this point, before it actually wilts, you will prevent permanent damage. Once a plant has completely wilted, it seldom fully recovers. It may perk up, but it will still have brown edges and poor growth.

Underwatering and overwatering can have the same symptoms. Consistently overwatering plants saturates the soil. The plant's tiny root hairs die. And because plants need air in the soil in order to absorb water, they wilt when soil is saturated. More water will not bring it back to life.

To know when plants are ready for water, check the moisture level of the soil. If a plant needs moist soil, the surface should be damp. If a plant should dry somewhat between waterings, the top 1 to 2 inches of soil can be dry, but if it's dry below this point, water the plant. Letting a plant dry out completely will damage the roots, sometimes beyond repair.

You may eventually get to a point where you know your plants well enough to lift a pot and from its weight know whether to water. You will learn which plants dry out most quickly, such as those in clay pots, south windows, or some potting mixes. Over time, adjusting your watering to accommodate your plants will become second nature.

THE BEST WAY TO WATER

For most plants, the best and easiest method is to pour water on the soil surface. Pour until water runs out the drainage holes, which also leaches salts from the soil.

A wick draws water up to the plant by capillary action. To start a wick system, poke heavy-duty, natural-fibered cording into the root ball; pot the plant; pulling the wick through the drainage hole, wet the wick and keep it wet by draping it into a water-filled bowl.

Healthy roots will be plentiful, firm, and white or cream-colored. You may even see root hairs. Unhealthy roots will be hard to see, soft and spongy, dark-colored, and may smell bad.

If dry soil has pulled away from the pot so that water runs down the sides without wetting the soil, immerse the entire pot in a bucket of tepid water. Let it sit for about 20 minutes, then drain.

A few plants, such as African violets, benefit from bottom-watering because water droplets mar their leaves. Set the pot in a saucer of water. Capillary action will draw the water into the soil. This method takes longer than top watering, but it keeps water off the leaves. Wick watering systems and self-watering pots are other ways to bottom-water.

However you water, it is essential that a plant not sit in water. After about 20 minutes, empty the saucer. If the plant is too heavy to lift, remove the excess with a turkey baster.

Unless you are growing a plant that is extremely sensitive to hard water, don't worry about using tap water. Use tepid water to avoid shock and possible root damage from extremely hot or cold water.

FERTILIZATION

Fertilization, like watering, doesn't need to be a mystery. All plants, regardless of type, need 16 nutritional elements to grow. Three of these elements, nitrogen, phosphorus, and potassium, are used the most.

WHEN TO FERTILIZE: Plants need less fertilizer in winter when they grow slower, and plants in low light need less than ones in high light. Generally, plants need the most fertilizer in spring and summer when growing rapidly, less in fall as growth slows, and none in winter. Exceptions to this would be plants growing under lights that provide uniform day length and light intensity.

Some gardeners feel strongly about fertilizing once a month; others prefer to use a dilute fertilizer solution with every watering. Still others fertilize only during the growing season, such as on May 1, June 1, and July 1. Use whichever method works for you, or whichever is easiest to remember.

WHAT TO USE: Many formulations of fertilizers are available. Whichever you use, follow directions on the label. Powders or liquids that you dilute with water are easy to apply and allow control over how much to give a plant. Slow-release fertilizers, designed to be mixed with potting soil, release nutrients over a long period, depending on temperature and moisture. Plant spikes are concentrated sticks of fertilizer that you push into the soil, where they slowly release nutrients. These are the least preferable formulation because they unevenly deliver nutrients to plants and are expensive to use.

Every fertilizer has an analysis number on the label, indicating how much nitrogen, phosphorus, and potassium it contains. Nitrogen fuels growth and leaf production, phosphorus stimulates root and flower production, and potassium helps develop sturdy, disease-resistant plants and aids fruit production. If you grow flowering plants, you may want to use a fertilizer with a higher phosphorus amount, such as 15-30-15. Foliage plants thrive on a balanced fertilizer, one in which the three numbers are the same, such as 20-20-20.

Regardless of the formula, always follow the directions on the label. If in doubt, use a dilute solution and adjust it as you see a growth response. It is better to slightly underfertilize than to risk damage or overstimulate a plant. In other words, more is not necessarily better.

Most fertilizers build up in soil over time, so it's a good practice to leach plants every 4 to 6 months. Simply run water through the soil several times to flush away fertilizer salts, then drain well.

The three numbers on a fertilizer label are the product's analysis and indicate the amount of nitrogen, phosphate, and potash in the bag. In a balanced fertilizer, the three numbers will be the same or nearly so.

6 FL. OZ.	(170ml)
7.5 OZ. NET WT.	(212 G)

Plant Food

10-8-7

GUARANTEED ANALYSIS

Total Nitrogen (N) 10%
  2.7% Ammoniacal Nitrogen
  7.3% Urea Nitrogen
Available Phosphoric Acid (P_2O_5) . . .8%
Soluble Potash (K_2O) 7%
Copper (Cu) 0.05%
  0.05 Chelated Copper
Iron (Fe) 0.13%
  0.13% Chelated Iron
Manganese (Mn) 0.08%
  0.08% Chelated Manganese
Zinc (Zn) 0.05%
  0.05% Chelated Zinc

Potential acidity equivalent to 350 lbs.
Calcium Carbonate per ton.
Chlorine - maximum available 5.5%

SOURCES: Ammonium phosphates,
Urea, Muriate of Potash, Copper
HEDTA, Iron EDTA, Manganese EDTA,
Zinc EDTA

SOIL AND CONTAINERS

Plants need an "anchor." There are elaborate hydroponic systems where the roots grow in water, but most plants need soil to hold them in place and provide nutrients.

Plant roots require air and water for health, so the mixture in which their roots reside must provide plenty of both. It must also retain moisture and nutrients for the plant's use.

Garden soils are generally too heavy for use in containers and bring with them problems of disease and insects. Many potting soils for indoor plants are soilless. These can be custom mixed according to individual plant needs, although commercial mixes available at your local garden store are fine for most plants.

Soil components vary according to the mix needed for specific plants. Clockwise, starting in upper left corner: perlite, sphagnum peat, coarse sand, calcined clay, charcoal, vermiculite, and bark chips in the center.

Most commercial potting mixes are composed of peat moss and vermiculite or perlite in various proportions. They are free of pests, diseases, and weed seeds. And they are inexpensive, simple to use, and widely available.

If you find you need a potting soil with other ingredients, you can mix your own or purchase a ready-made mix. Commercial potting soils for flowering plants have more organic materials, such as shredded bark or compost, that retain moisture, because flower buds are sensitive to water loss. Cacti and other succulents need a mix with sand or calcined clay (clay pulverized by heating) for extremely good drainage. Bromeliads and orchids need a coarse mix of bark chips, which provide plenty of air for the roots.

When choosing a soil, look for one that is of medium weight. Too light a soil, such as one that is all peat moss, will not adequately anchor a plant. Too heavy a soil, such as one of sterilized top soil, can cause drainage problems. If you are potting a very large plant that will not be repotted often or that has the potential to become top-heavy, mix in about one part commercial, sterilized topsoil to three parts standard potting soil for some extra weight.

CONTAINERS

The only two essential considerations when choosing a pot are how it drains and what the shape and size are in relation to the size of the

Containers come in every size and shape imaginable. Some have drainage holes; others do not. Some are glazed inside, some are glazed outside, and some are unglazed. This is a sampling of unglazed terra-cotta pots.

plant and its root system. Beyond that, selection is a matter of preference.

DRAINAGE: Good drainage is imperative. No matter what type of plant you are growing, the pot must have holes for drainage. When using a decorative glazed pot without drainage holes, you will need to put the plant in a pot that drains. Then slip it into the decorative pot onto an inverted saucer or small pot.

A common myth when potting in a nondraining pot is that putting a layer of stones or sand in the bottom will give the water somewhere to drain. Water moves from capillary action from large pore spaces to progressively smaller pore spaces. Water will travel down through the soil, and when it hits the interface between the soil and stones, it will stop and pool rather than continue downward into the stones. There is no substitute for a pot that drains well.

SIZE: When determining size, make sure your pot is large enough to contain plenty of soil to accommodate the root system and still leave an inch of room above the soil, called head space, for watering. A good design principle to keep in mind is that visually the pot should be no taller than one-third of the plant/container combination. Thus, a 9-inch pot would visually support an 18-inch plant. Flat, wide pots will hold water throughout the soil longer than deep, narrow pots, which quickly drain water away from the top half of soil. However, flat pots can cramp deep-rooted plants and stunt their roots.

PLASTIC: Pots come in a wide variety of materials, with plastic and terra-cotta the most commonly available. Both are fairly inexpensive, and there is an outstanding selection of decorative types available. Plastic pots are easy to handle, relatively unbreakable, and easy to clean and store. They keep the soil moist longer than terra-cotta but are sometimes too lightweight for top-heavy plants.

CLAY: Terra-cotta or clay pots are porous unless glazed, allowing air and moisture through the sides of the pot. Thus, soil dries more quickly in clay than in plastic. This is an advantage for cactus and succulents but may keep you on your toes with moisture-loving plants. Clay is breakable and harder to store but provides weight for stability.

SELF-WATERING: Self-watering containers, designed to provide water for extended periods, are used extensively in commercial settings. There are several types: pot-in-pot systems, wick systems, or vacuum systems with a reservoir that releases water as the roots break the vacuum. All self-watering pots keep the soil constantly moist, so plants that need to dry out between waterings don't perform well in them. Plants potted in self-watering systems need to be monitored, at least the first few weeks, to make sure the soil is not too wet.

Most self-watering pots have a reservoir in their bottom. As soil dries, it draws water from the reservoir.

To use a decorative container without drainage holes, pot the plant in a plastic container with drainage holes. Slip the plant and pot into the decorative container, elevating it on an overturned saucer.

SPECIALTY MIX INGREDIENTS

■ **AFRICAN VIOLETS, FLOWERING PLANTS:** Equal parts sand, peat moss, sterilized garden soil, leaf mold.

■ **EPIPHYTES, BROMELIADS:** Equal parts sphagnum moss, coarse bark, coarse perlite. Add 1 tablespoon dolomitic lime and 1 cup horticultural charcoal to 3 quarts mix.

■ **CACTI AND SUCCULENTS:** 2 parts sterilized soil, 1 part coarse sand, 1 part calcined clay. Add 2 tablespoons dolomitic lime and ⅓ cup charcoal to 4 quarts of mix.

■ **FERNS:** 3 parts peat moss-based potting soil, 2 parts perlite, 3 parts leaf mold. Add 1 cup charcoal to 2 quarts of mix.

■ **SOIL-BASED MIX:** 1 part sterilized soil, 1 part peat moss, bark or leaf mold, 1 part coarse sand or perlite.

INDIVIDUAL INGREDIENTS:
■ **SPHAGNUM PEAT MOSS:** Partially decayed plant materials mined from the bottom of peat bogs; acid pH, highly moisture retentive, no nutritive value.

■ **SPHAGNUM MOSS:** Plant matter harvested from the top of peat bogs. Fibers, longer than those of peat moss, decompose slowly. Used mainly to line baskets rather than in soil mixes.

■ **PERLITE:** Ground volcanic rock; moisture and nutrient retentive, lightweight; helps improves drainage.

■ **VERMICULITE:** Mica expanded by heating; moisture-retentive.

■ **SAND:** Lime-free, coarse river sand is best. Avoid beach sand; it contains harmful salts.

■ **SHREDDED BARK:** Finely shredded or ground hardwood or pine bark.

■ **CHARCOAL:** Use only horticultural grade; absorb salts and by-products of plant decay; keeps the soil sweet; removes acidity.

■ **LEAF MOLD:** Decayed leaves of all types; excellent organic additive for moisture retention; some nutrition.

POTTING AND DIVIDING

Surprisingly, many houseplants seldom need repotting. Some plants even perform better or bloom better if they are potbound. Other plants will need repotting if they outgrow their pots, if the soil has become depleted, or if the plant is infested with soil-dwelling pests. Repotting can be done anytime, but right before active growth starts in spring is ideal. Avoid repotting plants during a plant's dormant or resting period.

To determine whether a plant needs repotting, tap the plant out of its pot and look at the root system. A plant may have a few roots growing through the drainage holes, but if it's only a few, then repotting may not be necessary. However, if you pull an asparagus fern (and you will have to pull.) out of its pot, the root ball may be such a mass of fleshy roots that there is virtually no soil left.

Repotting will often rejuvenate a plant, especially if it is given a larger pot with more room for root growth and fresh soil. If a plant has outgrown its pot, you have the option of putting it into a bigger pot (potting up) or pruning the root ball and putting the plant back into its original pot. If you want the plant to grow bigger, move to a larger pot, but only 1 or 2 inches larger in diameter. If you pot a plant in a container that is too large, the pot will hold more soil and, in addition, more water than the plant can use. The plant may also spend all its energy forming roots, often at the expense of top growth.

If you want to keep the plant at the same size, tap it out of its pot, then slice off about an inch all around the root ball with a sharp knife. When you disturb the root system this way, you will need to prune some of the top growth at the same time. Otherwise, the plant will drop some of its foliage in response to losing its roots.

When a plant looks like it needs feeding but doesn't respond to fertilizing, it's probably time to replace the soil. If a plant needs its soil rejuvenated, you can replace part or all of the soil. For partial replacement, remove the plant, and knock off some of the old soil; tease the roots out a bit to encourage them to grow into the new soil, and then repot the plant. Or, scrape off the top inch or so and add new soil. This is the easiest way to replace soil around plants that resent having their roots disturbed, such as amaryllis. This technique is called dressing.

A well-potted plant is centered in the pot and given about an inch of "head room" for efficient watering.

Loosen the plant from its old pot and slip it out gently, taking care not to injure the plant.

Gently tease apart any tight or circling roots; loosen old soil gently with your fingers.

Clip any damaged or diseased roots. If returning the plant to the same pot, remove some healthy roots, too.

If the soil is completely depleted or you have an insect infestation, you need to remove as much of the soil around the roots as you possibly can. Tap off whatever soil you can, and then wash the roots with warm water. Examine the roots for any problems, prune out diseased or damaged areas, and repot.

STEPS FOR POTTING OR REPOTTING

1. Thoroughly water the plant several hours before repotting it.

2. Gather such supplies as a pot, screen to cover drainage holes, newspaper to cover your work surface, and potting mix.

3. Moisten potting mix to make it easier to handle. Potting soil is hard to wet after it's in the pot, but if done beforehand (even the day before), you can squeeze water through it with your hands.

4. Loosen the plant by running around the pot with a knife or tapping it on a table. Slip out the plant. For small plants, hold the top of the plant between your fingers, supporting the root ball in your palm. Larger plants can be removed by laying the pot on its side and sliding the plant out.

5. Unwind circling roots, cut off any that look rotted, and if the plant is pot-bound, make slashes through the root ball with a sharp knife. Cut off an inch or so of the root ball if you intend to put the plant back into the same pot.

6. Center the plant in the new pot, set it on the soil at the same depth as it was planted before, and fill in around roots with soil. Remember not to use stones in the bottom of the pot for drainage.

7. Tamp the soil lightly with your fingers as you work; pressing too hard will compact the soil. Water the plant well.

8. If the roots were pruned substantially, cut back the top of the plant accordingly.

DIVIDING

Division is an excellent way to rejuvenate a plant that has overgrown its pot and its setting. Not only that, you end up with one or more new plants. Plants with fibrous root systems are easily divided by removing the plant from its pot, cutting the root ball in half, and then potting each half. If you can pull apart the root ball, do so, but some plants are so dense that they will need a sharp knife or saw to split them. You can divide them into more than halves, but take care to only split them into pieces with plenty of roots.

Plants that produce multiple crowns, such as aloe, can be divided by separating the crowns into individual plants with roots attached. Repot them just like divisions.

To divide a plant, remove it from its pot, separate the leaves, and pull or cut apart the root ball. Center each section in a new pot, fill in with soil, and water well.

Center the plant in its new container, making sure the crown is at the same depth as in the old pot.

Fill in soil around the root ball, tamping and firming it gently with your fingers.

Water the newly potted plant thoroughly, allowing it to drain well into a saucer or decorative container.

PROPAGATION

Starting new plants from old is fun and rewarding. It's neither difficult nor time consuming in most cases. Propagation is a great way to develop healthy plants from an aging specimen, and many times it can even help to rejuvenate an older plant or aid in extending its lifetime.

STEM CUTTINGS

Select a healthy stem and take a 3- to 5-inch cutting with several nodes, where the leaf attaches to the stem.

Pinch or cut off the bottom leaves, leaving two remaining on the top of the cutting.

Dip the cutting into water and then into powdered rooting hormone. Tap off the excess.

Make a hole in the potting mix with a pencil or your finger; insert the cutting in the hole and firm the soil around the stem.

Water gently and cover the cutting with a plastic bag to retain moisture. Check after two weeks by tugging gently (a rooted cutting will resist).

OFFSETS

Remove the plant from the pot. Gently separate an offset (a small plant growing at the base of the parent plant) from the parent, cutting with a sharp knife, if necessary.

Plant the offset in potting soil at the same depth it grew in the original pot; tamp the soil lightly, then water. Give the offset the same culture as the parent plant.

PLANTLETS

Move the parent plant to a stable spot next to a separate pot of moist potting soil. Pin plantlets (small plants that grow from a stolon or leaf) to the soil in the neighboring with a hairpin or wire. Cut it away from the parent after it roots.

Another method is to cut off a leaf or stolon with plantlets attached and then pot it up directly. Pin the plant in place so it remains in constant contact with moist soil until it's established.

LEAF CUTTINGS

Remove an African violet leaf with its petiole (leaf stem) attached by clipping close to the crown of the plant.

Make a hole with a pencil in the potting mix. Dip the petiole in rooting hormone, then insert it in the hole, burying the entire petiole.

Firm the soil, then water thoroughly. Cover the pot with a plastic bag. Check every few days for new plants forming at the base of the leaf.

Cut a sansevieria leaf into 3-inch sections, making sure to keep them oriented upright. Making a notch in the upper end helps. Dip the sections in rooting hormone.

Stick the leaf cuttings into the potting mix, notched side up. Then firm the soil and water the cuttings. Cover the pot with a plastic bag.

PROPAGATION
continued

SEEDS

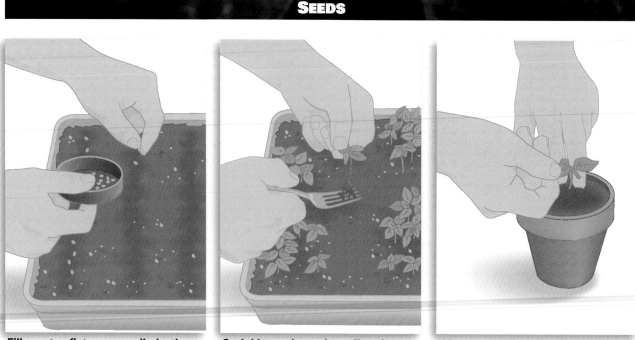

Fill a pot, a flat, or a small plastic tray with moistened, well-drained potting soil or seed-starting mix (vermiculite or milled sphagnum moss), and firm gently.

Sprinkle seeds on the soil surface, then cover with milled sphagnum moss. Water gently, cover the flat with plastic, and move it to a warm spot. Check daily for germination.

When seeds sprout, uncover the flat and move it into indirect light. Transplant seedlings to pots when they have their first set of true leaves, which look like mature leaves.

FERN SPORES

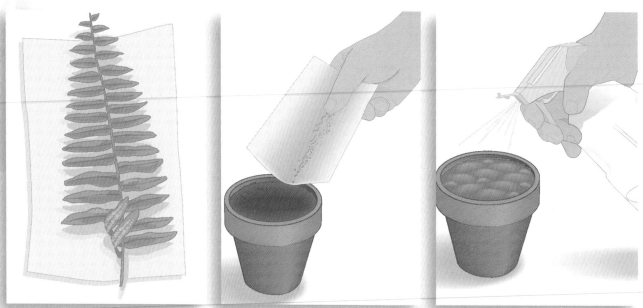

When tiny round bumps (spore cases) on the back of a frond have turned dark, lay the frond on white paper in a protected area. Spores will be deposited on the paper when they're ready for planting.

Prepare a flat or pot with moistened potting soil or seed-starting mix. Sprinkle spores on top of the mix, mist, and cover with a piece of glass or hard plastic. Check periodically to see if spores are germinating.

Be patient. New plants take a long time to develop. They go through a intermediate phase before turning into the form we're familiar with. When plants start to develop fronds, transplant them into small pots.

LAYERING

Move the parent plant to a stable location and place a pot with fresh potting soil next to it. Select a vining stem to layer.

Pin the stem to the soil at a node, leaving the growing tip free. When roots develop at the node, clip the new plant away from the parent plant.

AIR LAYERING FOR WOODY STEMMED PLANTS

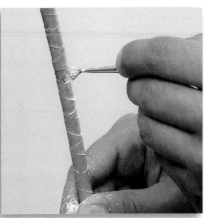

To propagate woody-stemmed plants, make a notch in the stem and remove the piece of stem.

Dust the notch with rooting hormone, then loosely wrap plastic around the stem, taping at the base.

Fill the plastic with dampened, long-fibered sphagnum moss.

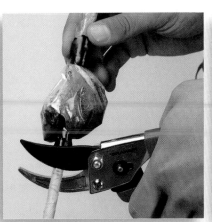

Close the top of the plastic with electrical tape or twist ties. Check daily to see if roots form.

After roots develop, cut the stem of the plant below the plastic. Remove the plastic and the moss.

Plant in fresh potting soil. Keep the parent awhile to see if it will sprout below the cut.

PRUNING

Pruning is one of the most rewarding aspects of plant care. Not all plants need it, but many benefit from pinching and heading back to stay shrubby and full. Some plants need a boost every once in a while, and pruning acts like a spring tonic. It encourages growth and corrects structural problems. It can direct growth so that a plant becomes a prime specimen. In some cases, pruning is essential to remove diseased or damaged wood or to reduce a plant's growth.

TOOLS

Before pruning, arm yourself with sharp, high-quality, bypass pruning shears. Although an investment initially, they will pay for themselves many times over by giving you clean cuts and allowing you to carefully control your pruning. Anvil-type pruners tend to crush the stem rather than slice it off, so stick with bypass types. Scissors can be used, but make sure they are very sharp. A plant stem that is crushed or torn by dull tools takes a long time to recover.

GOALS

When setting out to prune, try to keep in mind the overall form of a plant. The *main* reason for pruning is to make the plant look better, and careful work will leave it looking almost as if it was never pruned. There are some exceptions, such as when you need to cut a plant back drastically to reduce its size or cut off nonflowering wood. However, if you always have a reason to remove a branch, your plants won't suffer from the "bad haircut" syndrome. Remember, it takes a long time for a major stem that is cut off accidentally to be replaced. So, when in doubt, don't cut it off.

Other reasons for pruning are to remove diseased parts or to rejuvenate a plant. When removing diseased tissue, prune back into healthy tissue, always keeping in mind the overall shape of the plant. Dispose of the prunings immediately (don't leave them near the plant) and sterilize your pruners between cuts to avoid spreading disease by dipping them in a weak bleach solution.

If you are pruning to rejuvenate an aging or leggy plant, the plant's shape and growth habit should dictate how you prune. Remember, some plants do well with drastic pruning while others do not. It pays to know

A weeping fig needs periodic pruning to keep it always looking its best.

your plant well before you start cutting. The "Directory of Houseplants" beginning on page 58 can help.

HERBACEOUS PLANTS: Plants such as African violet and peperomia send up leaves from a flat crown and have basically a round, symmetrical shape called a rosette. Plants of this form will only need pruning to maintain an even shape. Remove older leaves from the underside of the rosette, pinching off the leaf and petiole as close to the base as you can. You should also remove any leaves that detract from the shape, such as misshapen or large ones.

Vining plants, such as Swedish ivy and pothos, will need regular "haircuts" to keep them in the peak of health. They produce new leaves on the ends of long stems, and regular snipping will keep the plant bushy and full by forcing new leaves to grow along the stem. Pruning them is a matter of cutting a stem just above a leaf joint or node. Try to clip the stems at uneven lengths to keep the plant from looking as if it just got a haircut.

Other plants, such as ming aralia and fishtail palm, naturally have irregular shapes and so will only need an occasional unhealthy leaf removed. Remember, if you don't have a good reason to cut something off, don't.

Stemmy plants, such as fibrous begonia and Swedish ivy, can and will benefit from the occasional severe pruning to force healthy new growth.

WOODY PLANTS: Norfolk Island pines, lemons, and other woody houseplants may need occasional pruning of an entire branch or part of a branch to look pristine. These plants have woody stems that will take much longer to grow back than herbaceous stems. Remind yourself of this before cutting off a branch.

Weeping figs have a distinct umbrella shape as they age, and pruning them while young to encourage this shape will help achieve it sooner. In other words, branches that point straight up should be pruned out entirely, and side branches need to be headed back to give the plant a symmetrical shape.

PINCHING

Pinching, one type of pruning, is often done with the fingernails rather than pruners. This is a method where the tip of a stem and the topmost few leaves are pinched out to promote growth of the side buds. Pinching is a great way to keep shrubby plants full from the center and robustly dense. In some cases, such as with coleus, you can pinch out flower spikes to keep the plant only in foliage.

ROOT PRUNING

A specialized type of pruning, root pruning, is occasionally used to hold back a plant's growth. A plant naturally grows new roots at a root cut or break, so deliberately pruned roots and the breaks that naturally occur when repotting will stimulate new growth. Severe root pruning is done to keep a plant in a small pot, although there are limits to how much of the root system you can remove without hurting the plant. Whenever you root prune a plant, also remove some foliage so the reduced number of roots won't be overtaxed by too much foliage.

To keep plants bushy and full, pinch the tips of the stems regularly. With your thumb and forefinger, pinch off the stem just above a leaf.

After pruning, the weeping fig looks refined and tidy. Wayward stems were pruned out, some stems were headed back, and dead stems and crossing interior branches were removed completely. This pruning will direct growth toward a more pleasing shape.

GROOMING

Anything goes as dressing for your plants. Match your decor or your plant's flowers with colored aquarium stone, river rock, polished cut flower stones, Spanish moss or whatever tickles your fancy.

Just as you need regular grooming, so do your plants. It doesn't take much time and makes the difference between having an attractive plant or one that looks neglected. Perhaps more important than making your plants look good, regular grooming keeps you in touch with your plants (literally.), providing an opportunity to catch and eradicate disease and insect problems early when they can be easily controlled.

The amount of time you spend grooming will vary according to the type of plant. Some plants naturally shed and will need more time than others to have their leaves removed and dead stems pruned out. A little time spent with your plants when you water, however, will reduce the need to do major work.

LEAVES

The most obvious first step in grooming is to remove old, dead leaves. If a leaf yellows, it won't green up again. Pull off the leaf. Some plants don't give up their leaves easily, so keep a pair of scissors handy rather than risking tearing the stem. (Leaves on nutrient-deficient plants turn pale green and yellowish. In this case, fertilize.)

Remove the entire leaf instead of trimming off brown parts. Trimming may make the plant look better temporarily, but the leaf will end up browning at the cut edge again, starting an endless cycle in which the final step is removing what's left of the leaf. Grit your teeth and remove it when it begins to brown. Chances are you won't miss it.

While you are removing dead or yellow leaves, make a determination whether they are being lost as a normal leaf shed or whether there is a cultural or pest problem. This is a good time to reassess the plant's cultural situation. Go over the plant thoroughly; you might save yourself some trouble down the road.

DUST

Next, get out your duster and take it for a spin. Even a little dusting can make your houseplants look their best. Dust makes a plant look neglected and can clog the leaf's stomates, preventing air exchange. If the dust gets heavy enough, it can even block light from reaching the leaf. A feather duster is the perfect tool to use for small-leaved plants, and large-leaved plants benefit from a gentle wipe with a soft cloth while you hold and support the leaf in your other hand.

Use a dry cloth to prevent making a muddy mess and having to go back to wash the leaf a second time. The only time you might need to dampen the cloth is if the dust is greasy. And if it is greasy, you will probably need to use a mild detergent solution to clean the leaf. If your water tends to leave white mineral deposits on the foliage, you may need a damp cloth to remove them.

When a leaf has faded, clip it off at the base. Leaving it on will only detract from the beauty of the plant.

ENHANCEMENTS

Once you clear away the dust, a leaf's natural shine will come through. There are plenty of "shine" products available, but in most cases, these use a sticky wax that can clog pores and make a dust problem worse. They also tend to make a plant look artificial, the last thing you want if you have a healthy, live plant. If you absolutely want more shine, try very dilute skim milk.

Plants sometimes benefit from a quick, yearly shower, although you may choose to shower them several times a year or never. Small-leaved plants that are hard to get with a duster respond well to putting them in the tub and rinsing them with tepid water. In good weather, you can do this outdoors in a protected area. Don't use too strong a spray from the hose. Warm the water in the hose by letting it lie in the sun before spraying the plant. Extremely cold water will shock even the toughest plant.

Each time you water a plant, give the pot a quarter turn. This lets all parts of the plant have access to the light and keeps it from getting lopsided. Plants grow toward the light (called phototropism), and providing light to all sides makes the plant fuller.

Fresh soil in a pot is a beautiful enhancement, but it doesn't stay fresh long. Use mulches to embellish your plants and containers, to keep things tidy, and also to help conserve moisture by slowing evaporation.

MULCH

Mulch is another easy plant enhancer. Although bare soil at the bottom of a plant looks great when the plant is first potted, it eventually begins to show fertilizer deposits and collect dead leaves and stems. Adding a mulch not only makes a plant look better, it reduces evaporation from the soil.

You can use anything to mulch—let your imagination go. Generally, something natural works best, but if you want to use aqua-colored aquarium stones to accent a blossom color, go right ahead.

The most common mulches are stones, sphagnum moss, sheet moss, calcined clay, sand, or Spanish moss. Peat moss is not generally a good choice because once it dries out, water rolls off the top of the moss, wetting the sides of the pot and not the soil underneath.

A superb, underused mulch is a ground-cover plant. Not only does it perform many of the same duties as other mulches, it also adds another texture to the planting. How about planting baby's tears or English ivy at the base of your weeping fig? Just be sure to choose a ground-cover plant that shares the same cultural requirements as the larger plant.

Turning your plants regularly keeps them uniform. If not turned, they will grow toward the light, becoming misshapen.

STAKING AND TRAINING

To stake or not to stake? Tying a plant to a post or stick is often necessary and functional, such as when helping a wobbly plant to stand up or when training a plant to grow in a particular direction. But staking and training go far beyond putting a stick in the soil and tying a plant to it.

There is endless opportunity for artistic expression with stakes, such as training a vine to a topiary form or natural arch, training plants into a living wall or curtain, or creating a sculpture that combines a plant with an imaginative trellis.

SOLVING PROBLEMS: A stake used to hold up a plant that has been poorly grown never accents the plant but rather accentuates the fact that the plant is lopsided or uneven. In these cases, it might be better to start over, drastically pruning the plant or tossing it altogether.

In some cases, a stake is necessary only to temporarily correct a problem , and once the plant has started growing well, the stake can be removed. In other cases, the stake is an integral part of the plant/pot combination, and is a permanent addition to the overall "look" of the plant.

Staking and training usually work best if you start with young plants. Older plants will have stems that don't bend quite as easily, while young plants not only are pliable but also can be pruned as they grow to cover their support. Training plants onto a form takes more maintenance time than growing other indoor plants, and may require at least a couple of years to develop an attractive plant.

WHAT KIND OF STAKE? When choosing a stake or support system, use one that is at least as thick as the stem you are supporting. Thin stakes bend and break, especially as the plant top gets heavier with new foliage. You can, however, use thin branches that are very flexible, such as willow or dogwood, in arches rather than as straight sticks. Tie the stems of your plants to the arch, lean the plant against the arch, or use two arches, one on either side of the plant.

Stakes made of natural materials or painted natural colors, such as green or brown, will tend to disappear when engulfed with foliage. Black is the least visible color. Green or tan bamboo stakes are readily available and inexpensive. They are amazingly strong and long lasting.

In addition to stick-type stakes, ready-made forms and trellises also are available. A trend is to use twigs and stems to create arches and trellises. There are also wire and wooden forms of all shapes for plant training.

Some plants must be staked, so use your creativity to make the stakes disappear or, at least, become part of the overall ambience of the plant.

WHAT ABOUT TIES? For tying the plant to a stake, again choose green or brown materials, such as twine, raffia, or even green twist ties or plastic tape. Remember that the wider or softer a tie, the less chance it will injure the plant stem. Tape is a good choice if the tie can't be seen. Because tape is wide and stretches, there is less chance it will girdle a stem if it is forgotten. If the ties will be visible, choose raffia or another natural fiber that will look as if it's part of the design. You can even use grapevine tendrils to loosely tie a plant.

When tying a plant to a stake, make the shape of a figure eight, with one loop around the stake and one loop around the plant. This allows the plant a little movement, which may prevent breakage. Tie loosely so there is plenty of room for an expanding stem.

Also, be sure to tie a plant in several places instead of just one. If the top of the plant is very full and heavy, tie it in several places to keep it secure. A plant stem is vulnerable to breakage where it is tied, and there's nothing more disheartening than to find a plant that has broken at its only tie.

Once you have a plant staked, it is critical to check the ties regularly. Plants grow fast, so you must make sure the ties are not girdling stems, that there is not a problem with disease under a plastic tie, and that the plant still needs its stake. If in doubt, take off the tie and retie it. It's a small amount of time spent to keep a plant looking good.

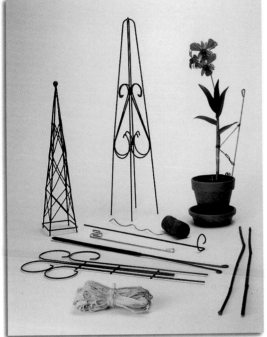

You will find all types of stakes and supports available commercially, although some of the most attractive support systems can be made from twigs and branches from your garden. Whatever you use, make sure it is sturdy and natural-looking.

TRAINING A STANDARD

A standard is a plant trained to a single stem—usually in a lollipop form. Indoor plants that lend themselves well to this type of training are those with strong or woody stems, such as coleus, flowering maple, geranium, lemon, calamondin orange, and ming aralia or rosemary.

Choose a well-rooted cutting or seedling with a single sturdy stem. Pot the plant in a heavy pot in well-drained, heavy potting mix. Tie the stem loosely at several intervals to a firmly seated stake, taking care not to bind the stem.

Pinch off side shoots, letting leaves remain along the main stem to sustain the plant. When the plant has reached the desired height, pinch out the growing tip to force side shoots for the main head. As side shoots develop, prune them to achieve the shape you want.

As the plant gains size and becomes more top-heavy, repot into a large, heavy pot. Depending on the plant you use, it may be possible at some point to remove the stake if the plant stem can stand on its own.

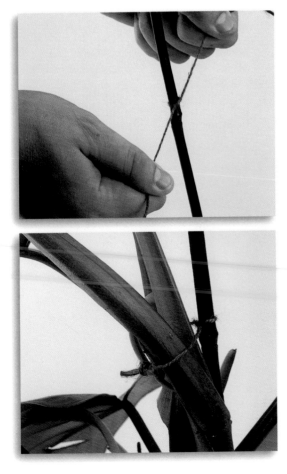

Use natural materials to tie plants to stakes. Make a snug loop around the stake and then a loose loop around the plant, creating a figure eight. This allows the plant stem some movement. Tie the plant in several places instead of one. With just one tie, the stem becomes vulnerable to breakage.

SEASONAL CHORES

In order to efficiently groom and care for your plants, keep this list handy for reminders of monthly chores.

JANUARY
Give plants a shower; adjust for short days.
FEBRUARY
Check for new insect outbreaks.
MARCH
Prune for spring growth.
APRIL
Repot if necessary.
MAY
Fertilize.
JUNE
Fertilize; move plants outdoors if desired.

JULY
Fertilize.
AUGUST
Inspect plants for insects. Prune where needed.
SEPTEMBER
Bring in plants; take cuttings of annuals for growing on the windowsill.
OCTOBER
Check carefully for pest outbreaks and control as needed.
NOVEMBER
Check humidity levels after you turn on the furnace.
DECEMBER
Move plants around as necessary to compensate for shorter day lengths.

PROTECTING YOUR HOME

Saucers make short work of watering and prevent messes. Non-porous saucers protect the surfaces of your furniture and woodwork and can actually enhance the look of a container, if chosen carefully.

No matter how beautiful your plants are or how attached you are to them, there is nothing that will dampen your enjoyment faster than a leaking pot that ruins your carpet, wood floors, furniture, or windowsill. Selecting the perfect pot is fun. Making sure that the pot won't ruin your house isn't. But it is necessary.

PREVENTING LEAKS: Luckily, there are saucers and trays designed to keep water from ruining your woodwork.

You can get clear plastic saucers, terra-cotta colored plastic saucers, saucers that attach directly to hanging baskets, copper windowsill trays, and all manner of decorative pots that are sealed against moisture loss.

Saucers, drip trays, and coasters come in a wide variety of styles and materials—from plastic and terra-cotta to ceramic and copper to stone and cork.

Even putting a container into a saucer may not solve the problem, because all materials can sweat if the humidity is high enough. A cork coaster dissipates moisture before it

collects at the bottom of the pot. A trivet lets water evaporate before it runs to the floor.

DRAINAGE: Don't fall into the trap of thinking that if a pot doesn't drain, it won't leak. It may still sweat, and if it doesn't drain, the plant will suffer. Always put your plant in a pot with drainage. Then, to protect your home, put the draining pot inside a specially chosen decorative pot. This "pot in pot" method allows water to drain freely into the decorative pot, keeping the water off your table or windowsill. Also, because the space between the two pots is wide enough to let water evaporate from inside, the outer pot usually doesn't sweat, either.

A common mistake is to assume that glazed containers are well sealed and will not leak. All it takes is one small flaw or crack in the glaze, and you will have a table ring. Some good principles to follow, regardless of the type of decorative container you use, are to put a plastic saucer inside the pot and to elevate the decorative pot on a trivet, cork coaster, or something else that will allow air underneath the pot.

PLACEMENT: Now that your pot is secure, it's time to decide where to put your plant. If possible, avoid areas that water can harm. Put your plant on a tile or linoleum floor rather than a wood floor. If you must put it on carpet, a wood floor, or windowsill, find a piece of linoleum or glazed tile to put beneath it. Single tiles are inexpensive and a great investment to keep your room protected. And if you eventually reach the point where you have a windowsill full of plants, why not tile the entire sill?

A tiled windowsill is one of the best and most decorative solutions to dripping plants.

HOUSEPLANTS OUTSIDE FOR THE SUMMER?

After a long winter indoors, houseplants benefit from being washed clean of dust by spring rains and having natural insect predators feast on the mites and scale that indoor plants always seem to have.

If you decide to move your plants outside, give them a slow acclimation process. Gradual acclimatization allows a plant to adapt to the environment outdoors, avoiding sunburn, wind tattering, and cold damage.

Tuck low-light plants under shrubs or trees in full shade and high-light plants where they receive a couple of hours of early morning sun and are shaded the rest of the day. Be sure to monitor moisture levels carefully. Take these few steps and then enjoy your plants as ornaments for the patio and garden.

To use a container without drainage, put your plant in a pot that drains, then set it in the non-draining pot.

Fill the void between the two pots with milled sphagnum moss. Or use Spanish moss.

Placing moss between the plastic pot and the outer container helps raise humidity around the plant.

A pot-in-pot lets you use a decorative container that lacks drainage holes, which protects your home.

WHY THINGS GO WRONG

We all love having plants around us, but it's easy to become complacent about their care. Houseplants don't usually take much care besides watering, dusting, and pulling off an occasional leaf. When they look just fine, it's easy to forget about them.

How often, though, when your plants have been doing well, do you notice that the Boston fern is shedding more leaves than usual, the hibiscus has more than a couple of yellow leaves, and the occasional fungus gnat flying around the hoya has been joined by a squadron? Problems like these need to be addressed before they get out of hand.

Brown tips on any plant indicate that a problem exists. It's your job to be a detective, discover what the problem is by assessing both the plant and your cultural practices.

ASSESSMENT

Integrated pest management (IPM) is a current, rational approach to keeping houseplants healthy. It gives the gardener a step-by-step approach to observing, assessing, and minimizing problems.

Plants often have mild infestations that are constant and tolerable. Although no one knows exactly why, when a plant is under stress, insect populations often balloon. A plant that does not have enough light, humidity, or air circulation may be under just enough stress to start the cycle of problems. Perhaps the plant is pot bound and can't get the water you give it. And when a few insects find themselves in the vicinity, they get a good hold and begin multiplying.

Once you know you have a problem, you need to evaluate the factors and then decide what options you have. You may have to decide whether the plant is even worth keeping. An IPM system will guide you to the most effective and least invasive methods for keeping your plants in top shape.

THE RIGHT PLANTS

A key factor in keeping your plants healthy is to choose plants that are right for your growing conditions. Nothing will heighten a problem faster than putting a high-light plant into a low-light situation. If you have a spot near a heat register, select a plant that tolerates hot, dry conditions.

Make sure that any plant you bring into your home is clean and healthy. Don't add plants that already have existing problems. Always check new plants carefully before placing them with others. It's helpful to isolate a new plant for a few weeks to see if a problem shows up.

Once the new plant is settled in, the most important condition to keeping it healthy is proper care. Healthy plants are amazingly able to resist problems. Make sure water, light, humidity, soil, and temperature are correct and you will get vigorous, trouble-free growth. Also, regular propagation for a steady supply of new plants will help. Youthful plants are naturally more stress free.

This begonia is obviously unhealthy. Through close observation and consideration about its care, you will discover a pattern of overwatering. The plant shows classic symptoms, which indicate that its roots are suffocating.

KEEP IN TOUCH

Make it a habit to look at and touch your plants every time you water. When you dust the leaves, check for signs of insects or disease. If you catch a problem early, chances are you can stop it much more easily than if you wait until the entire plant is infested.

If you find a problem, move the plant away from others and isolate it while you work on controlling its particular problem. Check the plants around it to see whether the infection or infestation has spread.

FIGURE IT OUT

The next step is to correctly identify the insect or disease. If you try to treat before diagnosing, you are wasting time and money and could harm the plant.

Be aware that insecticides don't control disease, and fungicides don't do anything to rid a plant of insects. And neither are solutions to cultural problems, such as nutritional deficiencies.

NOW FIX IT

Once you've identified the problem, learn everything you can about it so you can treat it appropriately. Usually, that means determining the life stage at which the pest is most susceptible to a control. Understanding the insect or disease life cycle will help you decide when and how to treat it.

For example, when dealing with scale insects, the early crawler stage—the first stage after hatching—quickly succumbs to low-toxicity pesticides, such as insecticidal soap, or to cultural controls, such as strong blasts of water. Once the scales develop a hard shell, though, you must physically scrape them off the plant, smother them with horticultural oil, or use a more potent pesticide, such as malathion or pyrethrin.

Unless you are extremely vigilant, however, it's unlikely you'll notice the crawler stage, and the plant will be covered with both crawlers and adult scales. That situation requires you to use a variety of controls over a longer period of time.

In some cases, control may not be feasible. For example, it's nearly impossible to eliminate spider mites. Often, the best way to deal with them is to toss the plant.

Start your research on houseplant problems and their control at the local extension office. In most offices, you can pick up handouts or consult a Master Gardener.

INTEGRATED PEST MANAGEMENT (IPM) FOR HOUSEPLANTS

■ Identify the problem.
■ Inspect the root system. Repot the plant, if necessary.
■ Isolate the plant to halt the spread of the disease or the insect.
■ If feasible, prune out heavily infested portions of the plant.
■ Wash off insects by spraying leaves, top and bottom, with tepid water.
■ Using your fingernails, tweezers, a tissue, or a cotton swab dipped in alcohol, pick or wipe off pests.
■ Wash the entire plant with insecticidal soap.
■ Spray with horticultural oil.
■ Apply an insecticide labeled to control the specific pest on indoor plants. Follow all directions and heed safety warnings.
■ Throw away the plant. Don't put it in the compost pile, where it might spread disease.

POOR CULTURAL CONDITIONS AND THE DAMAGE THEY CAUSE

■ **HIGH TEMPERATURE:** Weak soft growth, too-fast growth, flower bud drop, wilting, leaf drop.
■ **LOW TEMPERATURE:** Yellow leaves, bud drop, leaf drop.
■ **FROST OR COLD:** "Water-soaked" leaves, black leaves, wilting, leaf drop.
■ **NITROGEN DEFICIENCY:** Stunted growth, loss of vigor, leaves yellow, starting at the bottom of the plant.
■ **PHOSPHORUS DEFICIENCY:** Stunted, small leaves, older leaves with red or purple color.
■ **POTASSIUM DEFICIENCY:** Yellow margins around older leaves, yellowing between veins.
■ **TOO LITTLE LIGHT:** Weak, soft growth, older leaves drop, general yellow-green foliage.
■ **TOO MUCH WATER:** Leaf wilt, edema.
■ **TOO LITTLE WATER:** Leaf wilt, tip burn.
■ **LACK OF HUMIDITY:** Brown margins and tips.
■ **TOO MUCH FERTILIZER:** Leaf drop.
■ **TOO LITTLE FERTILIZER:** Lack of growth (may be desirable in some cases).
■ **SUNBURN:** Yellow to brown patches, sometimes white.
■ **SUDDEN ENVIRONMENTAL CHANGE (MOVE INTO LOW LIGHT):** Quick foliage drop.
■ **LACK OF PLANT ROTATION:** One-sided or lopsided growth.

WHAT CAN GO WRONG: INSECTS

Insect damage is fairly common on houseplants, especially since natural predators of pests rarely come inside. But they won't get out of hand if plants are in good health and have the care they need. If you follow the IPM monitoring steps carefully, you can keep any problems that develop within tolerable limits.

A FEW CLUES

Become familiar with the damage individual insect species do so you can employ some of the simpler methods for dispatching them.

YELLOWING LEAVES AND STIPPLING: Whenever a plant develops yellowing leaves, it's time to do some diagnosing. Leaves can turn yellow when plants are overwatered or underfertilized. But when it comes to insects, sucking insects are the most likely culprits. Their damage will appear on upper or lower sides of the leaf, and it will look more stippled than solid yellow.

Stippling—tiny yellow dots on the leaf surface—is caused by an insect inserting its proboscis into the plant and sucking plant juices. This not only weakens the plant, but may also transmit disease.

Because spider mites are probably the most common insect problem on houseplants, check for them first. They are too small to see easily, but their damage is distinct.

Take a piece of white paper, hold it under a leaf, and tap the plant. If the specks that fall

Mealybugs are soft-bodied insects that secrete a cottony white covering. They suck plant sap from leaf axils and branch crotches. New growth on a plant will be distorted, and the plant will be weakened. Mealybugs secrete honeydew, like aphids. Control by removing the white masses with a cotton swab dipped in rubbing alcohol or horticultural oil.

on the paper move, the plant has mites. If they don't, then it's dust.

STICKINESS: If you find a black, powdery substance on the leaves, it is most likely sooty mold, which grows on the honeydew excreted by sucking insects, such as aphids. If you find sooty mold, the plant has insects, so start looking. Sooty mold doesn't hurt the plant and can be washed off, but a heavy layer will

Whiteflies are flying insects that look like tiny white moths. If you shake the plant, they will fly up in a cloud and then settle back on the plant. Their damage is similar to that of spider mites. The leaves will be stippled and new growth stunted. Whiteflies must be controlled in the larval stage with insecticidal soap or oil. Adults can be trapped with yellow sticky traps.

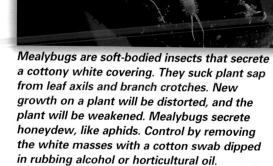

Aphids are soft-bodied insects, with or without wings, in red, yellow, green, or black. They suck plant juices from stems or leaves, distorting and stunting tips and leaves. Badly infested plants will drop their leaves. Aphids excrete honeydew, which leads to sooty mold, a telltale sign of aphids. Control by washing them off, spraying with insecticidal soap, or hand-picking.

slow light penetration, which prevents photosynthesis, and stresses the plant. Controlling the insects secreting honeydew will get rid of the sooty mold problem.

DISTORTION: Crinkled, twisted, stunted, or otherwise distorted foliage strongly indicates that something's wrong. Unfortunately, distortion can have many causes. Usually it means that the plant is not functioning as it should and that something is preventing the natural flow of sugars, water, and hormones to all parts of the plant. For example, a population of insects may be stopping the flow.

LEAF DROP: A plant may drop its leaves because it is not receiving water or nutrients from the roots. Again, look for insects, which may be plugging the flow.

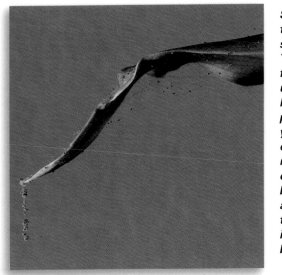

Spider mites are tiny insects that suck plant juices. They start out feeding on the undersides of leaves, but as populations rise, you find them all over. You may notice stippling or fine webbing between leaves and stems. By the time damage is visible, it may be extensive.

PREVENTION

If you notice a pest on one plant, chances are you will find it on its neighbors, too. You can't help but transfer insects from one plant to another as you dust and pinch.

The simplest way to dispatch most immobile pests is to hand-pick them from the plant. This may not sound like the most pleasant thing to do, but it does work. You can easily see larger pests like aphids, and it takes no effort to wipe them off with your fingers or a cloth.

Wiping down large-leaved plants regularly with a soft cloth gets rid of an amazing number of spider mites and whitefly larvae. A regular shower will also help rid the plant of many pests, as well as help it look its best by cleaning the leaves.

If you have a constant problem with spider mites, try boosting your humidity. Identify and correct any conditions that might lead to stress, such as poor air circulation, poor light, or lack of fertilizer. Shower the bottoms of the leaves for a day or two. In severe cases, you can try pruning off infested leaves and tips.

If you can't find insects on the stems or leaves, but still suspect pests, you may have root pests. Remove the plant from the pot to verify your suspicion. At this time, you can also remove the soil, rinse the roots, then repot the plant. This give you a chance to prune badly damaged roots.

For hard-to-control insects, remember that you can dispose of the plant.

Fungus gnats are small black flies similar to fruit flies. Adults are mainly a nuisance, but larvae feed on roots and can stunt plants. You'll see the adults flying; look for larvae when you water. If present in high numbers, they float. Because fungus gnats thrive in damp areas, control them by letting the soil dry out.

Looking like bumps on stems and leaves, scales are soft-bodied insects that suck sap from plants, then secrete a hard shell over themselves. Eggs develop under the shell. Later, tiny crawlers hatch and move onto the plant. At this stage, scales are vulnerable to insecticidal soap and oils. You can control the adults with oil also.

WHAT CAN GO WRONG: DISEASES

Diseases seldom bother healthy plants. While healthy plants may come under attack, they're better able to ward off the disease. On the other hand, houseplants that are constantly, or even periodically, stressed, are likely to develop disease problems. For example, letting a plant wilt before watering weakens the tissue, as does keeping soil too wet. And weak tissue is an invitation to disease.

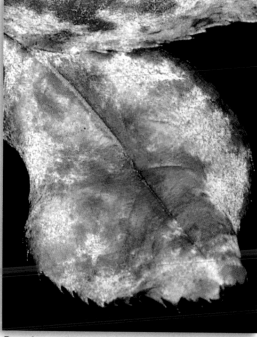

Powdery mildew, a whitish, powdery fungus, is seldom serious enough to kill plants. Still, it's important to eliminate it. Mildew indicates poor air circulation, high humidity, or overly moist soil. Improving growing conditions and removing affected leaves help correct it.

Viruses usually show up on all parts of a plant with quite distinct symmetrical markings. The only cure is to discard the plant.

PREVENTION

Regular grooming will prevent many problems. Immediately getting rid of leaves or stems that show signs of trouble is a good practice, regardless of the cause. Also, don't let dead leaves lie on the soil. It's easy to pick them off and toss them in the pot for "mulch." However, if those leaves have a disease, even in the very early stages, you are giving the disease a perfect nursery atop that moist soil. Put the leaves in the garbage.

IMPROPER CULTURE

Some diseases, like powdery mildew, indicate that your culture is improper in some way. Although powdery mildew isn't usually fatal, it is a beacon that conditions are right for something that can cause major problems to come along. By improving air flow, lowering humidity and temperature, decreasing watering, and pruning out diseased leaves, you can fend off powdery mildew and other more serious diseases.

Rot caused by fungi is an indicator of wet soil. It's not that wet soil kills the plant, but rather that excess moisture stresses the plant, and the pathogens get a foothold in the dampness and then proliferate. Letting the soil dry out will slow the growth of the disease, and the plant may recover if not seriously damaged. Pruning out diseased tissue can sometimes work, but if the rot is infecting the entire root system, you will probably have to discard the plant.

Leaf spots are caused by plant pathogens that enter a plant when it is stressed. It's seldom critical to diagnose exactly which leaf spot your plant has, and it would take a

Leaf spots appear as rings and holes in the leaves, and range from circular to irregularly shaped, in red, brown, yellow, or green. Most are caused by fungi, although some are bacterial. Leaf spots are best pruned out. Few other controls work on most houseplants.

pathology lab to do so, at any rate. Pruning or cutting out the offending leaves will often alleviate the problem, as long as you also correct the cultural problems that are making the plant prone to disease in the first place.

VIRUSES

Viruses are insidious infectious disease agents that are present in certain plants all the time in a dormant state. Most of the time, you will never see evidence of them. However, once a plant containing a virus is stressed, the virus may become active, distorting, stunting, and disfiguring a plant. Viruses often require a professional lab to diagnose. Often they are spread by insects, such as mites, aphids, and scales, so controlling these pests will prevent the virus from spreading.

Tobacco mosaic virus (TMV) affects many species and can be spread by exposing plants to tobacco smoke or by touching plants after handling cigarettes. There is no cure for viruses, so once a plant is badly infected, the only solution is to discard the plant. Luckily, viruses are usually specific to one or two species, so they don't get out of hand easily.

FUNGUS

Fungal disease develops when spores contact plant tissue and take hold. Moisture—on the leaves or in the soil—promotes disease development. The spores send out tentacles called hyphae into plant tissues, which they use to take sustenance from the plant, destroying the tissue in the process.

Often, what you see of the disease—leaf spots, rotted roots and other areas, or powdery residue—is evidence of the fungus reproducing and making new spores. With a microscope, you can often pick out the spores.

You can prevent many fungal diseases. First, eliminate sources of infection. Clean up fallen leaves and other debris that can harbor pathogens. Make the situation inhospitable for spore survival. Don't mist plants, and keep leaves dry. Second, use a fungicide. Fungicides work only as preventives, however, and not as cures. So, with fungal diseases, it is critical to start out with a healthy plant.

BACTERIA

Bacterial diseases, although not very common, do occur, and if left alone can kill a plant. The most common type we see on houseplants is bacterial leaf-spot disease. Bacteria are parasites like fungi, and they damage the plant by rapid, explosive reproduction that clogs plant tissue. Bacterial diseases are best prevented by purchasing healthy plants. They are also often spread by sucking insects, so make sure you carefully control them.

If you suspect a bacterial problem, try pruning out the diseased leaves, making sure to sterilize your pruners with alcohol between cuts. Some antibiotics are available, but they are often difficult to obtain. In most cases, it is wiser to discard the plant.

Rots occur on stems, crowns, or roots. Affected areas are soft and may have an odor. Let soil dry, prune rotted parts and discard plants that don't improve.

When roots are rotted by bacterial or fungal disease, the plant cannot take up water and the top wilts. Death will occur unless the problem is corrected.

WHAT CAN GO WRONG: POOR CULTURE

Tip burn means that the tips of the leaves have dried out. Regardless of the plant, the leaf margin begins to yellow and then brown and dry, often crumbling off. Water is not reaching the margins because the plant is overwatered, underwatered, or the humidity is too low.

Sunburn occurs when leaves receive too much sun. Brown to white patches appear and may cover the entire leaf. The plant may look bleached. Sunburn occurs because of seasonal changes in light, from moving the plant to a site with higher light, or from a water droplet on the leaf acting like a magnifying glass.

Your plant doesn't look quite right, but the symptoms don't fit any of the pest or disease explanations or pictures. What can it possibly be? Chances are that your plant has some sort of mechanical— or culturally caused—problem.

Many mechanical problems are easily solved once you know what you are dealing with. Few are devastating to the plant, as long as you catch them early enough.

The difficulty with diagnosing mechanical problems is that their symptoms frequently look alike. For example, a plant with yellowing leaves may be receiving too much water or too little nitrogen. Here are more symptoms to watch for.

WATERING SYMPTOMS

Suppose your geraniums on the window sill develop small, corky blisters or calluses on the leaves. On some of the leaves, the blisters have fallen out, leaving holes. You see no insects, and the problem is only on some of the leaves, indicating it's not a problem throughout the plant.

Your geraniums have edema. This is a classic problem that occurs on thick-leaved plants that have been overwatered or grow in unusually high humidity. The cells burst from too much water, and they heal over as corky spots. Although it's not possible to heal the damage, you can prevent further spots by correcting your watering habits.

Another classic watering symptom is tip burn. This happens on many plants, especially those with long or large leaves, such as spider plant and areca palm. Tip burn can be caused both by under-watering and overwatering. Correct your watering and you will prevent the problem from occurring on more leaves.

FERTILIZER SYMPTOMS

Symptoms of overfertilizing can show up on the plant, the pot, and the soil. On the pot and soil, it appears as

Fertilizer deficiency shows up as yellowing of the leaves. Many plants don't need to be fertilized often, and so may never have these symptoms. However, in extreme deficiency, a plant will begin to drop its leaves.

nutrients. Leaves may turn yellow, bluish, or purple, or develop brown spots. Correct fertilizer overload by repotting the plant, then flushing the soil with water.

The other side of fertilizer overload is nutrient deficiency. If the plant is deficient in nitrogen, leaves turn pale yellowish-green, and the plant grows slowly. A lack of iron results in a plant with dark green leaf veins separated by yellow tissue.

LEAF DROP

Weeping figs are a classic example of plants sensitive to change in the environment. Any alteration in humidity, temperature, or light can cause their leaves to drop. Usually, the plant will stop losing leaves as soon as it has become adjusted to its new environment.

Other houseplants will drop their leaves when subject to prolonged hot or cold drafts from outside doors opening and closing, excessively dry air, or exposure to gas or furnace fumes. If your plants are dropping leaves and you haven't recently moved them, reexamine the site to see whether it's really appropriate for the plant.

These are only some examples of the mechanical or physiological damage that can occur on plants. More are listed in "Poor Cultural Conditions and the Damage They Cause" on page 45.

a white, dry, chalky crust or powder. This crust is a layer of fertilizer salts. You frequently see it on pots of plants that haven't been repotted for several years. But if you routinely mix in more fertilizer than the label directions say to use, mix it with less water than directed, or if you fertilize with every watering, the crust will build up faster.

On plants, signs of overfertilization show up as browned leaf tips and edges. The salt buildup actually prevents the plant from taking up water, which is why the symptom is the same as for underwatering.

You can prevent fertilizer salt buildup by once-a-month leaching. Run clear water through the soil several times, then let it drain.

Fertilizer overload is a problem that occasionally develops. Some plants may take up more of one nutrient than others. For example, overloads of manganese, boron, and nitrogen are common in African violets. The overload, in turn, creates an imbalance of the other nutrients, and the plant develops deficiency symptoms for those

Teeth marks are usually signs of pets or children. Chewing produces irregular holes with tearing and scraping, but leaf spots will look fairly regular.

SOLUTIONS

You've diagnosed your problem, and now you need a solution. To find the appropriate treatment, read as much as you can and consult the Master Gardeners at your local extension office.

You may find that the problem is simply poor culture, such as overwatering. Then, the solution is also simple—reduce watering, let the soil dry out, and train yourself to check the soil before automatically watering. If you tend to underwater plants, you just need to be a little more disciplined and tuned in to their needs. Or, replace them with plants such as cactus that can survive your type of care.

If the problem results from a lack of humidity, try growing the plant on a pebble tray, in a pot-in-pot with sphagnum moss, or put a humidifier in the room. Misting a plant is not an effective way to raise humidity.

For a plant receiving too much light, move it or hang a sheer curtain between the plant and the window. Too little light is easily corrected by adding supplemental light or moving the plant closer to the window.

For poor air circulation and accompanying high humidity, install a ceiling fan or a portable fan. Also separate plants to forestall the transfer of diseases and insects and to increase air flow between them.

It's easy to build a good first-aid kit to help your plants through insect and disease problems. In addition to pesticides, keep these items on hand: A feather duster to keep plants free of pore-clogging dust, alcohol and cotton balls or swabs to dispatch mealybugs and some scale insects, baking soda to dilute in water as a defense against some fungal diseases, and insecticidal soap and horticultural oil to eliminate many insect problems.

PLANT FIRST-AID KIT

When it comes to insects and diseases, learn everything you can about their life cycles, the cultural conditions favoring the pests, and appropriate methods of control. You'll need to know the stage at which it's easiest to eliminate the pest, whether changing the environment can help, and the correct pesticide to use. Be aware that it sometimes takes several sprays to eliminate some insects because eggs continue to hatch after the adults die. Your local extension office should be able to supply this information.

Insecticides containing malathion and pyrethrum control many houseplant pests, but be aware that some brands are not registered for use on indoor plants. Check the product label; it should state whether you can use it indoors on houseplants to control the specific pest.

In addition to pesticides, your pest-control arsenal should include a feather duster to keep dust down and plants looking their best, soft cotton cloths for wiping foliage, swabs and alcohol for physically removing mealybugs and scale insects, and insecticidal soap, horticultural oil, baking soda, and dish detergent for making insecticidal sprays.

OTHER CONTROLS: Insecticidal soaps are biodegradable materials that are nontoxic to humans, animals, or birds. They are made of fatty acids that penetrate the body of an insect, disrupt its metabolism, and kill the pest. They work only by contact. Most soft-bodied insects are vulnerable to the soap, although it may take several applications for complete control.

Before use, check the label to ensure the soap is appropriate to use on your ailing plant. Set the plant on a waterproof cloth or in the

Leaf pores are easily clogged with dust, so a regular shower helps remove the dust and some insects as well. If the weather permits, take plants outside and rinse them with a garden hose (if your water is not frigid). In winter, put the plants in the bathtub and give them a shower.

bathtub. Mix the spray (or use ready-mixed) and test the soap on a few leaves to check sensitivity. If there is no adverse reaction after 30 minutes, coat the plant with the solution. Keep it away from direct sunlight until the soap dries to prevent burn.

Horticultural oils are also biodegradable and nontoxic to mammals and birds. They operate by smothering an insect or by entering its cells and interfering with its metabolism. Oils are effective on soft-bodied insects as well as on hard-shelled scales. They work by contact, leaving no residual effect; therefore, it may take several sprays for complete control.

You may have heard that baking soda helps prevent fungal diseases, such as powdery mildew and black spot (on roses). The usual dosage is 1 tablespoon in a gallon of water with 1 teaspoon dish detergent, which helps it stick to the leaves. However, baking soda as a disease control is still under investigation. No dosage specific to houseplants has been determined, so you may be taking a risk if you use it.

Whatever control you use, be sure to read label directions carefully and follow all precautions. It's especially important to spray the undersides of leaves because that's where many insects dwell. Repeat application if the problem persists.

Exposure to high, direct light and a clear window can cause problems from sunburn to tip burn or spider mite infestation because of dry conditions. Exposure to a window in winter can cause chilling or even freezing injury. If you have this type of situation, consider installing a sheer curtain to give the plants some gentle protection. The curtain can easily be adjusted as necessary during the day to let in more or less light and more or less warmth.

A fan to circulate the air around your plants goes a long way toward reducing the incidence of fungal diseases. The moving air evaporates the moisture layer, reducing the chance that fungal spores will take hold. Too strong a stream of air, however, will drastically reduce your humidity.

BUYING HOUSEPLANTS

Only take home healthy, robust plants unless you're looking for a challenge and plenty of extra work.

Now that you've decided exactly which plant you want to add to your home, it's time to get out there and pick one. Before you go, make sure you know everything you can about the plant so you can make the wisest choice.

WHERE TO BUY

It seems houseplants are available in every corner store, to say nothing of plant specialty stores. You find them at booths at conventions and county fairs, in hardware stores, grocery stores, in tents on busy corners, delicatessens, and at farmers' markets.

Although you may find perfectly fine, healthy plants at all of these places, one thing you usually will not find is someone who is knowledgeable about houseplants. If you purchase from anywhere other than a plant shop, you must be aware of the risks of a plant being mislabeled, mishandled, or unhealthy.

For the best selection and the best access to information, go to plant specialists. These may be greenhouses that specialize in houseplants, botanic gardens that have plant sales, florists, or garden centers. When you visit a plant supplier, trust your instincts. If the place feels good and smells good, and plants look healthy at first glance, chances are you've found a good supplier. If the place is a mess or if many plants seem unhealthy, you'd be better off looking elsewhere. You may not always want to buy expensive plants at specialty plant suppliers, and there's no reason why you can't pick up an occasional plant at the grocery store. Just be aware that you will need to make an extra effort when you buy, and you may end up with a real bargain. Remember that when you purchase your plant at a convention booth or in the hardware store, you seldom have the opportunity to return the plant if it is not satisfactory. You will also seldom find anyone who can answer a question about a plant's care.

TAKE A CLOSE LOOK

When you are in the plant store and have a likely candidate, pull it away from the other plants, into good light, and look it over very carefully. Sometimes sales personnel rush to assure you that all their plants are pest free, but it is essential to look for yourself. Remember that any plant that has been repeatedly stressed is a candidate for insect and disease problems.

Look at the soil first. Make sure there is no moss or fungus growing on the soil and that there is no sign of fertilizer salt buildup. These all indicate poor culture. Brown leaf tips or edges are signs that the plant may be stressed. You may feel silly, but smell the soil. A sour or "off" smell can indicate root or crown rot or overwatering. Also, a strong pesticide smell may indicate that the plant was infested. Look extra carefully for insects. In fact, you may want to come back in a week to check it again before taking it home.

Look at the leaves to make sure that they are full size and the right color. Check all parts of the leaves, including top and undersides, petioles, and leaf axils. Even if you don't see any insects, make sure there is no sooty mold or sticky honeydew. Check carefully for webbing, and then pull out a piece of white paper and tap a leaf over it to check for spider mites. If you find insects that you don't recognize, check with the sales personnel. In many instances, commercial greenhouses use predatory insects to keep pests under control. This is good!

LIST OF GIFT PLANTS

Amaryllis
Azalea
Christmas pepper
Chrysanthemum
Cyclamen
Cineraria
Florist's gloxinia
Persian violet
Poinsettia
Primrose

Appraise the form of the plant. You want one that is appropriately stocky and thick for its type. Don't take a plant with poor form or that is leggy and thin, because this is an indication that the plant wasn't grown well. A plant that has been pruned or staked to make the form better should be suspect.

PROTECT YOUR INVESTMENT

When you feel sure that you have chosen an almost-perfect plant, the last thing you want to do is damage it in transit. In summer, even though the temperatures are moderate, you must still protect the plant from wind and sun. One of the most common causes of plant death during transportation is leaving the plant closed up in a car in the sun. Also, you must make every effort to avoid its being whipped by wind or burned by sun coming in the windows. Wind not only tatters leaves but also can desiccate them, causing them to fall off. Protect plant leaves near a window with newspaper or a blanket.

In winter, cold damage is quick and lethal. Plants need only a very short exposure to temperatures below 40° F to be permanently damaged. Plant sleeves are the most common method of protection, but they are intended only for short trips. Warm the car before loading the plant.

The more insulating warm air you can get around a plant, the less risk you take on your trip home. Although paper sleeves are better at insulating than plastic sleeves, try placing the plant in a large plastic bag, fluffing it with air and tying it closed securely. A closed cardboard box is another alternative.

GETTING SETTLED IN

When you have your plant safely home, you will need to acclimate it to its new setting. If you picked up your plant from a greenhouse, it was most likely growing in ideal conditions. Although you may have a perfectly appropriate spot as its new home, the plant will still need to acclimate to the conditions in your house.

It's wise to isolate the plant for at least a few days to double-check that it has no disease or insect problems that you missed. If you are providing very different conditions than it was grown in, you will be wise to introduce it to its permanent home gradually. Put the plant in a high-light area for a few days and let it adjust. Then gradually move it to lower light. Be ready for some reaction to the change, such as leaf drop or elongation between nodes.

BRINGING A POINSETTIA BACK INTO BLOOM

If you want to bring your poinsettia back into bloom, you must pay careful attention to the dark period it needs to force coloring. Keep your poinsettia well watered and in a sunny windowsill through the early spring. When danger of frost has passed, prune it back to only two or three leaves per stem and then put it outdoors in a partially shaded spot. While it's outdoors, pinch it regularly to keep it full and shrubby. Pinch for the last time around September 1, about the time it should be brought indoors and put on a bright windowsill. Beginning October 1, give the plant uninterrupted darkness for 14 hours a day. It is important that the plant not even be exposed to a streetlight or lamplight. The best way to fulfill this need for darkness is to put the plant in an unused closet from 5:00 p.m. until 7:00 a.m. In the morning, move the poinsettia back to its sunny windowsill. Continue this regimen until the bracts begin to color, usually around December 15. If you can also provide night temperatures of around 60° F, you will have brighter bracts that will last a long time.

GIFT PLANTS

Gift plants, such as cyclamen, amaryllis, azalea, and gloxinia, are always popular. And if you love a challenge, you can attempt to keep them alive or even bring them back into bloom. Other gift plants, such as cineraria, chrysanthemum, Persian violet, and ornamental peppers, will only bloom again in a greenhouse. You might consider discarding these rather than becoming endlessly frustrated.

Always protect your plants carefully when taking them from a warm, humid greenhouse or plant shop. For quick transport, plastic or paper sleeves work quite well.

HOUSEPLANT RESOURCES

RESOURCE LIST

BOOKS

Andersen Horticultural Library's
   Source List of Plants and Seeds
Chanhassen, MN: U. Minnesota
Library Publishing. 1993

Exotica
Alfred Byrd Graf. New Jersey:
Roehrs Company, Publishers. 1982.

Gardening by Mail
Barbara J. Barton. Boston:
Houghton Mifflin Company. 1997

Hortica
Alfred Byrd Graf. New Jersey:
Roehrs Company, Publishers. 1992.

Hortus III
New York: MacMillan Publishing
Company. 1976.

Indoor and Greenhouse Plants
   (2 volumes)
Roger Philips and Martyn Rix. New
York: Random House. 1997.

The Indoor Garden
John Brookes. New York: Crown
Publishers. 1986.

The New Royal Horticultural
   Society *Dictionary of Gardening*
Editor Anthony Huxley. London:
MacMillan Press, Ltd. 1992.

Once Upon a Windowsill—
   The History of Indoor Plants
Tovah Martin. Portland: Timber
Press. 1988.

The Royal Horticultural Society
   Encyclopedia of House Plants
London: Century Publishing. 1987.

Tropica
Alfred Byrd Graf. New Jersey:
Roehrs Company, Publishers. 1981.

WEB SITES OF INTEREST:

Indoor Web Ring—a ring of web
pages dedicated to indoor growing
www.globalnode.com/i__plants/

Interiorscape—Florida Plants online;
resources for indoor gardeners
www.floridaplants.com/interior.htm

MISCELLANEOUS

American Orchid Society
6000 S. Olive Avenue
West Palm Beach, FL 33405-4159
561-585-8666

HousePlant Magazine
P.O. Box 1638
Elkins, WV 26241

Saintpaulia & Houseplant Society
33 Church Road, Newbury Park
Ilford, Essex, England IG2 7ET
011441815903710
Quarterly bulletin
Annual subscription: £4 single

PLANTS

William Dam Seeds
P.O. Box 8400
279 Highway 8 (Flamborough)
Dundas, ON, Canada L9H 6M1
905-628-6641, fax 905-627-1729
email: willdam@sympatico.ca
Houseplant seeds

Davidson-Wilson Greenhouses
RR 2, Box 168
Crawfordsville, IN 47933
765-364-0556
www.davidson-wilson.com
Catalog $3.75

Glasshouse Works
Church Street, P.O. Box 97
Stewart, OH 45778-0097
740-662-2142, fax 740-662-2120
Orders: 800-837-2140
www.glasshouseworks.com
Tropicals, selected perennials; catalog
$2 for two years

Kartuz Greenhouses,
   Sunset Island Exotics
1408 Sunset Drive
Vista, CA 92083-6531
760-941-3613, fax 760-941-1123
Gesneriads, begonias, flowering
tropicals, subtropicals, vines

Lauray of Salisbury
432 Undermountain Rd., Rt. 41
Salisbury, CT 06068-1102
860-435-2263 email: jbecker@li.com
Catalog: $2

Logee's Greenhouses
141 North Street
Danielson, CT 06239
860-774-8038, fax 860-774-9932
www.logees.com

Lyndon Lyon Greenhouses, Inc.
14 Mutchler St.
Dolgeville, NY 13329
315-429-8291
www.lyndonlyon.com

McKinney's Glasshouse
P.O. Box 782282
Wichita, KS 67278-2282
316-686-9438, fax 316-686-9438
email: gesneriads@aol.com
Gesneriads, rare and exotic tropicals,
supplies

Merry Gardens
P.O. Box 595
Camden, ME 04843
207-236-9064

Northridge Gardens
9821 White Oak Ave.
Northridge, CA 91325-1341
818-349-9798
email: NorGardens@aol.com
Succulents, hard-to-find items

Oak Hill Gardens
P.O. Box 25
37W 550 Binnie Road
Dundee, IL 60118
847-428-8500
www.orchidmall.com/oakhillgardens/
Specialty plants, orchids, supplies

Rainbow Gardens Nursery &
   Bookshop
1444 E. Taylor St.
Vista, CA 92084-3308
760-758-4290, fax 760-945-8934
Plants and books; plant catalog: $2;
book catalog: free.

Trust your instincts. A display of healthy-looking plants will feel (and smell) right. Look for plants without disease or tip burn, with only natural shine instead of patent leather leaves from leaf polish, without salt buildup or fungus on the soil, and without signs of insects or their damage.

RESOURCE LIST *(continued)*

Sunrise Nursery
13105 Canyon View
Leander, TX 78641
512-267-0023
email: snrsnrsy@flash.net
www.flash.net/—snrsnrsy
Succulents, cactus; catalog: $1, refundable with order

Tiki Nursery
P.O. Box 187
Fairview, NC 28730
828-628-2212
Gesneriads (African violets)

SUPPLIES
Eco Enterprises
1240 N.E. 175th St., Suite B
Shoreline, WA 98155
800-426-6937
www.ecogrow.com
Growing supplies, lighting

Diamond Lights
1701 4th Street
San Rafael, CA 94901
415-459-3994
www.diamondlights.com
High intensity lighting, indoor growing supplies

Hydro-Farm
755 Southpoint Blvd.
Petaluma, CA 94954
707-765-9990
www.HYDROFARM.com
High intensity lighting, indoor growing supplies

Indoor Gardening Supplies
P.O. Box 527
Dexter, MI 48130
734-426-9080
www.indoorgardensupplies.com
Growing supplies

*An indoor garden, a collection of your favorite houseplants,
is one of the greatest joys you can have in your home.
Understanding each plant will help you keep your garden in
prime shape.*

DIRECTORY OF HOUSEPLANTS

Now comes the fun part. You have all the information you need for taking care of your plants, for selecting a good and appropriate plant for your particular environment, and for getting it home safely. It's time to choose the perfect plants to enhance your home and your life. This directory will give you specific information on each plant, including its individual cultural needs, its growth habit, how to propagate it, what pests to be on the watch for, and other tips.

If you want to choose a new plant, we've provided plenty of color photos to peruse. Before you get too excited about a particularly beautiful plant, though, make sure you match the plant's cultural requirements with your home's conditions.

For specific information about culture, we've listed the moisture, light, temperature, potting, and fertilization requirements for each plant. As we said earlier, choosing the right plant for the right place in your home is the key to success. If you have any doubts about the conditions in your home, check the chapter, "Right Plant in the Right Place," page 10, for tips about deciphering the climate within your home.

If your plant has a problem and you are doing some troubleshooting, be sure to read the chapter "Growing the Best Plants," page 26, for tips on cultural problems, and then check the directory for pest problems for each plant.

We've included the methods to propagate each plant if you are so inclined. For details on each propagation method, read "Growing the Best Plants." Many people enjoy propagating their plants and passing them on to friends and family as gifts.

Finally, you will find some tips on each plant's idiosyncrasies. Knowing all the details and quirks of your favorites will help you maintain the most attractive, healthiest plants possible. The better you know them, the better they will do.

TAKING THE MYSTERY OUT OF SCIENTIFIC NAMES

Often, the common name of a plant is not enough for correct identification. A plant may have several common names, and to confuse things further, one common name can represent more than one plant. This is why botanical names are so useful—they leave no doubt as to which plant is which. Every plant has only one botanical or scientific name (usually in Greek or Latin), recognized throughout the world by horticulturists, botanists, and others in the plant industry.

Plants are most often classified by their flowers and fruits, although other characteristics may be used. Related plants are grouped into families and given a family name recognized by the ending *-aceae*. For example, *Aloe barbadensis*, medicine plant, and *Aspidistra elatior*, cast-iron plant, are in the Lily family, *Liliaceae*.

Individual plants are given a two-part name, consisting of a genus and specific epithet. A genus is a group of plants with similar broad characteristics, and the genus name is the noun that describes them. For example, weeping fig, *Ficus benjamina*, and fiddle-leaf fig, *Ficus lyrata*, are both in the *Ficus* genus. The second part of the name, the specific epithet, is an adjective that distinguishes the members of a genus from each other and often describes a physical characteristic of the plant. Together, the genus and specific epithet comprise the species name. Fiddle-leaf fig has the specific epithet *lyrata*, which refers to the plant's lyre-shaped leaves. Combined with the genus name *Ficus*, the plant has a species name of *Ficus lyrata*. Species names are always written in italic or underlined.

Some plants within a species may have a naturally occurring variation, indicated by the abbreviation "var." for variety. An example is *Codiaeum variegatum* var. *pictum*. This is the brightly colored croton we are all familiar with. The species *Codiaeum variegatum* has leaves that are colored green and white. Its variety *pictum* has naturally red and yellow variegation. (It is equally correct to leave the word "var." out of names, for example, writing them as *Codiaeum variegatum pictum*.)

A variation that is developed and cloned by humans, is called a cultivar (short for cultivated variety), and it's name is enclosed by single quotes. The cultivar name may be descriptive of the characteristic or may identify the person who created the cultivar. Sometimes it is a combination of a descriptive name with some fun thrown in. *Cryptanthus bivitattus* 'Pink Starlight,' for example, is an earth star with bright pink leaves.

If a plant is a hybrid, either naturally occurring or man-made, the plant genus and specific epithet will be connected by an "×" to indicate that the plant is the result of cross pollination. For example, *Abutilon × hybridum* stands for a hybrid flowering maple. Christmas cactus, *Schlumberga × buckleyi*, is the result of a number of crosses.

Although plants are grouped taxonomically (classified) by characteristics that they share and are named accordingly, we have informally grouped some of the plants in this

THE ANATOMY OF BOTANICAL PLANT NAMES

The convention of giving plants two-part botanical names is called binomial nomenclature (binominal: two names, nomenclature: name calling). How the two names come together is depicted below:

Species name	=	Genus Kind (noun)	+	Specific Epithet Appearance (adjective)		
Ficus lyrata		*Ficus*		*lyrata*		

Naturally occurring variation of species	=	Genus	+	Specific Epithet	+	Variety (var.) (Natural variation)
Codiaeum variegatum var. *pictum*		*Codiaeum*		*variegatum*		var. *pictum*

Human-developed variation of species	=	Genus	+	Specific Epithet	+	Cultivar (Cultivated variety)
Cryptanthus bivitattus 'Pink Starlight'		*Cryptanthus*		*bivitattus*		'Pink Starlight'

Hybrid of species (natural or human developed)	=	Species Genus	+ ×	Species Specific Epithet		
Abutilon × hybridum		*Abutilon*	× (Hybrid)	*hybridum*		

encyclopedia by habitat, meaning that they will require similar cultural conditions. For example, bromeliads are grouped together because they are epiphytes and require special growing conditions to accommodate their particular root system.

We have grouped desert cacti together because of their need for high light and arid conditions, ferns because of their shared requirement for moist, humid conditions, and seasonal cacti because they are all forest cacti that grow as epiphytes in moist rain forests.

The source for binomial nomenclature in this book is *The Royal Horticulture Society Index of Garden Plants.* Taxonomists often change plant names to reflect recent research, so names may be changed even as we print this book. We have made every attempt to use the most recently accepted names.

REGIONAL DESCRIPTIONS

Once you have a proper scientific name, it's an easy task to use the myriad resources available to locate more information on a plant's origin. Knowing a plant's origin will assist you greatly in deciding what kind of care it needs.

A plant may be listed as having an origin as specific as the rain forests of Peru, meaning that it has fairly individual cultural needs and requirements. Other plants may be listed as native to tropical America and Asia, giving them a broad range of tolerances. The climatic regions listed below are general but should give you some broad guidelines for selecting plants.

■ Amazon basin, rain forests of Central America, western Africa, East Indies: warm and rainy all the time; moderate to low light.
■ Most of South America, Central America, Caribbean, southern Florida, most of Africa, Southeast Asia and the Philippines, northern Australia: well-defined wet and dry seasons; hot, humid summers; warm, humid winters.
■ Southwestern United States, northern Mexico, Australia, central and east Africa, southwestern Asia: high temperatures, high evapotranspiration rates, high light, infrequent rains, soil with poor nutrient-holding capacity.
■ Central Chile, Mediterranean (southern Europe, northwestern Africa), south and southwestern Australia, South Africa: hot, dry summers; cool nights; moderate, humid winters.
■ Southeastern United States, southeastern South America, eastern China, eastern Australia: warm to hot, humid summers; cool to mild winters; substantial precipitation all year-round.

■ North-central China, central Asia, U. S. Great Plains, southern and western Argentina: wide range of temperatures with hot, dry summers and cold, dry winters.
■ Western Europe, Britain, Pacific Northwest, New Zealand: humid, warm summers and humid, mild winters; large amounts of rainfall.
■ Northern United States, northern Asia and Europe: cold winters with snow, moderate to warm summers with average amounts of rain.
■ Japan and Ryukyu Islands: strong temperature contrasts; cold, dry winters; summer monsoons.

WHAT DO LATIN WORDS MEAN?

Latin may seem frightfully obtuse, but learning what some of the descriptive words mean will take you a long way toward understanding plant names. Some words may seem a little far-fetched, especially when a plant is named for someone, but others are straightforward and accurately describe the plant.

Alba	White
Albiflora	White flowers
Argentea	Silver, silvery
Aureum	Golden yellow
Bifurcatum	With two forks
Brevifolia	Short leaves
Densiflorus	Densely spaced flowers
Elastica	Elastic, returns to original when bent
Elegantissima	Elegantly
Fragrans	Fragrant
Fruticosa	Shrubby, bushy
Hybridus	Hybrid
Japonica	Japanese
Leuconeura	White nerved
Lyrata	Lyre or fiddle shaped
Marginata	Edged
Microphylla	Tiny leaves
Miniata	Flame scarlet
Pendula	Pendulous
Phyllostachya	Spiky leaves
Pictum	Painted
Podophyllum	Footlike leaf
Pulcherrima	Beautiful
Pumila	Small, dwarf
Purpuratus	Purple
Recurvata	Curved backward
Reflexa	Bent abruptly backward
Rhombifolia	Rhomboid-shaped leaves
Scandens	Climbing, twining
Stolonifera	Having stolons or runners
Tomentosa	Covered with dense, short hairs
Trifasciata	Marked with broad stripes of color
Variegatum	Variegated

PLANT DIRECTORY

ABUTILON X HYBRIDUM

Flowering Maple

Malvaceae

The flowering maple, also called Chinese-lantern or parlor maple, was a standard fixture in Victorian parlors because it was easy to grow and bloomed all spring and summer. The plant is native to most tropical regions of the world, making it an extremely adaptable houseplant, and it is a vigorous grower—up to several feet a year. The plant has large, maplelike leaves in varying shades of green or variegated with white or yellow. The medium-size pink, red, or yellow flowers hang down on thin stems like earrings, looking very much like small hibiscus flowers. Because of its popularity, many hybrids have been bred, often with large, multicolored flowers.

MOISTURE: Provide plenty of moisture, keeping the soil evenly moist during the flowering season. Reduce water in winter, letting the top 2 inches of soil dry out between waterings.

LIGHT: Medium-to-bright light is fine; it will bloom best if given direct light or sunlight

'Souvenir de Bonn' flowering maple

filtered through curtains. The plant tends to stretch and stop blooming in a low-light situation.

TEMPERATURE: Average temperatures are best. Put in a cool location in winter.

FERTILIZATION: Fertilize monthly with regular-strength fertilizer March through August, using 10-30-10.

PESTS: Watch for mealybugs and aphids.

REPOTTING: Flowering maple blooms best when slightly pot bound. The roots fill a pot quickly, so the plant may need repotting annually if its growing situation is ideal. Repot in winter or early spring. Pot in a moisture-retentive mix made especially for flowering plants.

PROPAGATION: Cuttings from stems or shoots before they mature or seed.

TIPS: Cut the plant back to half its size in fall to ensure a bushy, full plant the following year. In early spring, cut the tips back slightly to keep the plant full and producing abundant flowers. This is a fairly large plant, so give it plenty of space. Prune it to shape in the dormant winter period. Turn the plant regularly to keep it growing symmetrically. Most plants tend to be somewhat upright, although there are cultivars that droop and look spectacular in a hanging basket. Although they will fall off by themselves, you will have a nicer looking plant if you remove the spent flowers and flower stalks regularly.

AESCHYNANTHUS LOBBIANUS (A. RADICANS)

Lipstick Plant

Gesneriaceae

Lipstick plant

There's nothing quite so striking as a lipstick plant in full bloom, with clusters of bright scarlet, lobed flowers standing upright in every leaf axil. The base, or calyx, of each flower, which actually resembles a lipstick tube, is purplish. The thick, leathery leaves are sometimes edged with red, and lend a pleasantly tidy look to the plant. Native to the humid tropics, lipstick plant must have plenty of light and humidity to continue to bloom, but it also needs a rest period in the winter.

MOISTURE: Water well and keep the soil moist during blooming season; cut back on water in winter. Be sure to let it drain thoroughly. Put the plant on a pebble tray to increase the humidity.

LIGHT: This is definitely a high-light plant, but avoid direct sunlight.

TEMPERATURE: Provide average-to-warm temperatures during blooming, and cool temperatures in winter.

FERTILIZATION: Once a month at regular strength during blooming season, using 10-30-10. Don't fertilize in winter.

PESTS: Mealybugs or aphids may be a nuisance.

REPOTTING: Repot only every two to three years, as the roots fill the pot. Small plants may take a few years to fill a good-size basket. Use a mix that is half African violet mix and half epiphyte mix.

PROPAGATION: Stem cuttings taken before they mature.

TIPS: As soon as the plant stops flowering, cut back the stems to avoid its getting leggy. These plants are best displayed in hanging baskets. Don't hesitate to prune back the stems hard. Although sometimes hard to bring back into flower, it still makes a striking plant even when only showing foliage. Some types, in fact, are grown only for their beautiful foliage. If you have good luck with lipstick plant, there are other Aeschynanthus species to try that have orange, pink, or yellow flowers.

AGLAONEMA COMMUTATUM

Chinese Evergreen

Araceae

Chinese evergreen is one of the best low-maintenance plants. It almost always looks good with little fussing. The long, strappy leaves come in a variety of sizes, shapes, and variegations. When growing well, it will produce white spadix-and-spathe flowers, much like a flamingo flower (*Anthurium*). This plant is native to Southeast Asia and the Philippines.

MOISTURE: Allow the soil to dry slightly between waterings; don't let the plant stand in water because its roots are prone to rotting.

LIGHT: Chinese evergreen does well in low light, although it will also perform well in medium light.
TEMPERATURE: Average temperatures.
FERTILIZATION: Infrequently—once a year is probably enough in low light. Fertilize more often in high light with 10-10-10.
PESTS: Relatively disease and insect free. Mealybugs may appear at base of leaves, and spider mites may appear in bright light and dry conditions.
REPOTTING: In low light it seldom needs repotting. Use an average potting soil when necessary.
PROPAGATION: Stem cuttings, division.
TIPS: Keep out of cold drafts. Force new growth by removing long canes.

Chinese evergreen

ALOE BARBADENSIS (A. VERA)

Medicine Plant

Liliaceae

The healing sap of this familiar medicine plant, with its light green, spongy leaves speckled with white, has been used for centuries to treat wounds.

MOISTURE: Allow soil to dry out between soakings. Don't let plant stand in water.
LIGHT: As high light as possible. Direct sunlight is fine.
TEMPERATURE: Average temperatures are best. Hot or cool temperatures do not adversely affect plants.
FERTILIZATION: Fertilize three times in summer with an all-purpose 10-10-10

fertilizer. Do not fertilize plants in winter.
PESTS: Virtually pest free, but you may occasionally see a mealybug or two. If the plant is kept too wet, root and crown rots can quickly destroy it.
REPOTTING: Seldom needs repotting unless the roots are obviously pushing their way out of the pot. Use a potting mix designated for cactus.
PROPAGATION: Offsets, division, and seed. Separating the offsets is the easiest method of propagating.
TIPS: Because it is armed with teeth along the leaf margins, do not place a medicine plant where it can reach out and grab unsuspecting passersby. Pruning is not necessary except to remove damaged or faded leaves.

Medicine plant or aloe vera

ANTHURIUM

Flamingo Flower

Araceae

Flamingo flower is known for its spadix-and-spathe flowers. (A spadix is a floral spike and a spathe is a bract that shields it.) Most have bright red, yellow, or white flowers that sit atop tall, wiry stems. Leaves are shiny and dark green with distinct veins. Flamingo flowers are native to tropical America, including Hawaii, and the Caribbean.

MOISTURE: Allow the soil to dry slightly between waterings, but keep the plant surrounded with high humidity by providing a pebble tray or humidifier.
LIGHT: Low to medium light is best.

TEMPERATURE: Average temperatures; flamingo flower tolerates high temperatures, too.
FERTILIZATION: Fertilize three times in summer only, using 10-30-10.
PESTS: Mites can be a problem in low humidity; occasionally aphids.
REPOTTING: Repot when stems begin crowding the pot, and watering is difficult. Use a mix of half standard potting soil and half epiphyte mix. Good drainage is key.
PROPAGATION: Division, rooted side shoots, or seed.
TIPS: Keep flamingo flower out of drafty spots and out of high-traffic areas because the exotic leaves and flowers are easily damaged. Prune only as needed to remove old leaves.

'Cotton Candy' Flamingo flower

ARAUCARIA HETEROPHYLLA

Norfolk Island Pine

Auracariaceae

Norfolk Island pine, native to Norfolk Island in the South Pacific, is a splendid evergreen tree. Tiny specimens are often used in terraria, and medium to tall plants up to 5 feet make striking accents that look unlike any other type of plant. They are a popular choice as living Christmas trees. The feathery, tiered branches are covered with spiny, stiff, bright green needles.

MOISTURE: Keep the soil moist during active growth, but do not let the plant stand in water. Let the top few inches dry out between waterings. Moderate humidity will help the plant hold onto its lower branches.

LIGHT: Medium to bright, indirect light.

TEMPERATURE: Tolerant of a wide range of temperatures. Keep somewhat cool in winter.

FERTILIZATION: Fertilize infrequently to restrict growth, using 10-10-10.

PESTS: Mealybugs and spider mites.

REPOTTING: Repot infrequently to restrict growth. Use a standard potting mix.

PROPAGATION: Hard to propagate without elaborate facilities.

TIPS: These plants naturally lose lower branches, so prune them out cleanly when necessary. If using for a Christmas tree, avoid using lights (they dry it out) or ornaments that are too heavy for it.

Norfolk Island pine

ASPARAGUS DENSIFLORUS 'SPRENGERI'

Asparagus Fern

Liliaceae

This delightfully ferny plant is standard for use in hanging baskets, indoors and out. It's quite possible to use one plant in both places if you acclimate plants when moving them outdoors or indoors. The species is native to South Africa, and is tolerant of heat and dry conditions.

MOISTURE: Keep the soil evenly moist.

LIGHT: Medium light; plants are tolerant of high light as long as temperatures are cool.

TEMPERATURE: Average to cool best, but plants take short periods of high temperatures.

FERTILIZATION: Unless you want to inhibit the plant's growth, fertilize with a dilute solution every time you water using 10-10-10.

PESTS: Spider mites can be a problem, and watch for aphids on new shoots.

REPOTTING: The bulbous roots will bulge out of the pot when it's time to repot, and watering will become very difficult. Use a standard potting mix.

PROPAGATION: Division, seed.

TIPS: Asparagus ferns shed leaves fairly regularly, so shake out the plant to get rid of them once a week. Keeping the soil evenly moist and the plant in cool conditions helps prevent shedding. Otherwise, prune out fronds as needed to keep the plant attractive. Be careful when pruning because the stems have thorns.

'Sprengeri' asparagus fern

ASPIDISTRA ELATIOR

Cast-Iron Plant

Liliaceae

This is called cast-iron plant for a reason. It is the ultimate houseplant for the houseplant "neglecter." It remains stalwart and attractive even when forgotten and left without water for weeks. Its long, elegant, dark green leaves are held on short stems, emerging straight up and then gently drooping as they mature. Its origin in central Asia and the Himalayas indicates that it will tolerate a very wide range of conditions.

MOISTURE: Allow soil to dry between soakings. Average humidity is fine.

LIGHT: Low to high light; these plants continue to grow with almost no light (although it's not advised) but grow best in medium light.

TEMPERATURE: Average-to-cool temperatures.

FERTILIZATION: Don't fertilize.

PESTS: Mealybugs are probably the worst insect problem, and spider mites can proliferate on the undersides of the leaves in dry situations.

REPOTTING: Repot only when you want the plant to put on new growth. Use a standard potting mix.

PROPAGATION: Division.

TIPS: Although this plant will take abuse, if given good conditions it will be a beauty. It's an excellent choice to use where you just want something green in a dark area.

Cast-iron plant

BEGONIA

Begonia

Begoniaceae

This group of plants contains a vast array of interesting leaf shapes, colors, and textures, not to mention an outstanding variety of flowers. Some gardeners have only begonias for houseplants, and there are so many types available that they still have an incredibly diverse and beautiful display. Many can be set outdoors on a shady patio during the summer. Begonias may be short and stout, pendulous and drooping, or upright and stiffly elegant. Some begonias have large, bright, double flowers of red, yellow, or white. Others have tiny, airy, pale pink or cream flowers that delicately accent the large, distinct leaves. Many of the types grown only for their foliage will still bloom if given enough light. Begonias hail from all over the tropics and subtropics, so they have a wide range of cultural needs, dependent on the species.

MOISTURE: Keep the soil evenly moist for all begonias. Average humidity is fine, as long as the air circulation is good. Do not overwater, as this may lead to crown rot.

LIGHT: Most begonias thrive in medium light, although some may need higher light to bloom well. Many of those grown strictly for foliage will do well in lower light, and some are accentuated by a plant light.

TEMPERATURE: Average house temperatures are usually adequate, but beware of drafts.

FERTILIZATION: Fertilize with a dilute solution at every watering during active growth. Don't fertilize during winter. Use 10-30-10 if you want flowers, and 10-10-10 for foliage.

PESTS: Mealybugs can be a problem; watch for leaf spots (prune out problem leaves).

REPOTTING: Repot annually and use an average, well-drained potting mix.

PROPAGATION: This depends on what type of begonia you are trying to propagate. Fibrous-rooted begonias and rhizome-producing begonias (the largest group of begonias) can be easily propagated by division. Tuberous begonias may be propagated by tip or stem cuttings, or by division of the tuber. The large-leaved begonias propagate well by leaf cuttings or division. Because many types tend to look ragged after a few years, propagate them regularly to keep your house filled with attractive plants.

TIPS: Begonias are prone to leaf spots, so provide good air circulation and avoid getting water on the leaves. They do not tolerate drying or cold drafts. Most begonias should be pruned immediately after they finish flowering. Regular attention, in the form of pruning and pinching, will help to keep them dense and attractive.

Rex begonia

Angel wing begonia

'Rhizo' begonia

'Iron Cross' begonia

BRASSAIA ACTINOPHYLLA (SCHEFFLERA)

Umbrella Plant

Araliaceae

Umbrella plant is a good, solid houseplant that has stood the test of time for one good reason: It is reliable. Plants grow quite large, so be sure you have the room to allow for healthy growth. Alternatively, there are dwarf cultivars. The palmlike, shiny green leaves of umbrella plant start tiny but can grow to 10 inches across. Native to Queensland, in northeast Australia, it tolerates varying conditions.

MOISTURE: Keep soil evenly moist during active growth, but spare the water in winter. Water only enough to keep the potting mix from drying completely.

LIGHT: Medium light produces the best growth, although plants will tolerate less light.

'Arboricola' umbrella plant

TEMPERATURE: Average home temperatures are most appropriate, although the plants tolerate hotter conditions. If the plant is used in a hot situation, be sure to avoid drafts.

FERTILIZATION: Fertilize three times in summer, and then do not fertilize all the remainder of the year unless you want to push it to grow.

PESTS: Mealybugs can be a serious problem and hard to control by physical removal because there are so many small leaflets. You may also find scale, mites, and aphids.

REPOTTING: Repot only as the plant outgrows its pot and then use an average potting mix.

PROPAGATION: Stem cuttings, air layering.

TIPS: Prune plants as needed to keep them looking good. You may find that you never have to prune them at all, but if you do, they tolerate it well.

To keep the plant in control (smaller than a small tree) pot it in no larger than an 8-inch container. Replenish some of its soil regularly. To keep the plant looking its best, remember to clean the leaves regularly with a dry, soft cloth. The shiny leaves of umbrella plant will lend a shimmering tropical air to any room.

CALATHEA PICTURATA

Peacock Plant, Second-Chance Plant

Marantaceae

Peacock plant is native to Brazil and so enjoys high humidity and hot summers. Tuberous, clumping plants, it has leaves colorfully marked with purple, red, or burgundy undersides and purple to red stems. Peacock plant is often confused with the prayer plant, but their growth habits are completely different.

MOISTURE: Through the spring, summer, and fall, keep the soil evenly moist. Growth slows as winter comes, preparing the plant for a rest period. Continue to keep the humidity high but reduce watering. Tuck the plant out of the way until new growth begins in spring (just don't forget it!).

'Argentea' peacock plant

LIGHT: Peacock plant thrives in medium light and will also usually do well in low-light conditions.

TEMPERATURE: Provide average home temperatures. It tolerates hot spots as long as the humidity is high; it often does really well during hot, humid summer days.

FERTILIZATION: Fertilize only three times in summer using 10-10-10.

PESTS: Watch for mites and mealybugs.

REPOTTING: Before the plant becomes root bound enough to limit water uptake, repot in an average, well-drained potting mix.

PROPAGATION: Division.

TIPS: Peacock plant is fairly tough, but if by some chance the leaves dry out, you get a second chance. Remove the dead leaves, adjust the cultural conditions and healthy new growth should appear quickly. Some calathea species are challenging to grow, but once you've had success, you'll be hooked. It is definitely worth at least a couple of tries to add this colorful beauty to your home collection. As the plant approaches its rest period, it begins to look a big ragged, indicating that it's time to tuck it out of the way. As soon as you see new sprouts, prune out the old leaves and water well. Before you know it, your peacock plant will be showing off its beautiful plumage again.

Bromeliads

Bromeliaceae

Bromeliads are unlike most other plants because many of them are epiphytic. In their native habitat, they use trees, rocks, and other plants for physical support. They have minimal root systems, and draw their sustenance from water and pockets of soil collected by their roots and the "vases" formed by the leaves.

They often grow high in the canopy of the rain forest. Because of this unusual habitat, bromeliads need an extremely well-drained medium in which to grow. They can be grown on slabs of bark or in mixes of loose bark. If you grow one on a slab, you must provide high humidity to mimic the conditions in which they are found in nature.

MOISTURE: Allow the potting mix to dry out between waterings, but keep the "vase" filled with water.

LIGHT: Provide the highest light possible.

TEMPERATURE: Bromeliads thrive in average to hot temperatures.

FERTILIZATION: Fertilize three times in summer using 10-30-10.

PESTS: Watch for scales and mealybugs.

REPOTTING: Pot in an epiphyte mix. Repot only when the potting mix itself begins to break down.

PROPAGATION: Separate offsets.

TYPES OF BROMELIADS

LIVING-VASE PLANT (*Aechmea fasciata*) Living-vase plant has thick, spined, bluish to gray leaves, sometimes streaked with silver and white. Its flowers are actually large spikes of purple-to-blue bracts that contain the true flowers of red or purple.

TIPS: When the main flower has faded, the plant develops side shoots. When these shoots are about 6 inches tall, prune out the main "vase" to keep the plant growing.

VASE PLANT (*Billbergia*) Native to the tropics and subtropics, vase plant has long, strappy leaves and purple to red flowers accompanied by colorful pink or purple bracts that last a long time. Each vase dies soon after it flowers but is replaced quickly by another vase or two.

TIPS: For best results, remove the flowering vase as soon as the flower fades and the vase begins to yellow.

EARTH STAR (*Cryptanthus bivittatus*) Earth star is a terrestrial bromeliad, grown for its outstanding leaf colors of pink, green, and silver. The plant is small and flattened, and is particularly well suited for dish gardens or light gardens.

TIPS: Propagate earth star by removing offsets and potting them up even before they develop any roots.

PINEAPPLE DYCKIA (*Dyckia brevifola*) Dyckia is also a soil-dwelling epiphyte that is particularly tough and tolerant of neglect. It is stiff, almost resembling cactus, and has remarkably beautiful leaves with stripes and scales both underneath and on top.

TIPS: Place where the spiny leaves won't be damaged or won't damage passersby.

*'Silver Vase'
living vase plant*

Earth star

Water bromeliads by filling the vase with water and letting the potting mix dry somewhat.

Pineapple dyckia

Cactus
Cactaceae

Pincushion cactus

Cactus, long used to lend a southwestern flair to a room's decor, is mostly native to the southwestern United States and Mexico as well as to arid parts of South America. Its leaves have been modified by evolution into spines, reducing their evapotranspiration rate (water loss) considerably. Most cacti are covered with a waxy epidermis, further reducing water loss. Cacti are easy to care for and grow in the home, as long as you remember not to water them.

MOISTURE: Allow the soil to dry out almost completely between waterings and withhold water in the winter to allow a cooling, dormant period. High humidity can cause problems, such as leaf scarring and rotting, so be sure to keep them dry and maintain good air circulation.

LIGHT: Provide the highest light possible. Direct sun is advantageous.

TEMPERATURE: Cool to hot temperatures are fine for most types of cactus. Most cactus do best if kept in bright light in summer and in winter. For the cactus grown for its flowers, this cool winter period is necessary to force them into bloom.

FERTILIZATION: Fertilize three times in summer only using 10-10-10.

PESTS: Root mealybugs are the most troublesome. Root rots and crown rots can be a problem if the plant is kept too moist. Also watch for scales.

REPOTTING: Pot in a cactus mix. Repot only when the roots seem to be pushing out of the pot or the stems reach the sides of the pot. To repot a spiny cactus, wrap a piece of thick cloth or carpet around the cactus, slide it out of the pot and quickly into its new pot.

PROPAGATION: Seed, stem cuttings, offsets.

TIPS: Cactus are seldom pruned, although segmented ones, such as bunny ears, can be separated for propagation.

TYPES OF CACTUS

BARREL CACTUS (*Echinocactus grusonii*) Barrel cacti literally look like little barrels with prominent ribs that are covered with intense-looking golden spines. It is slow growing and tolerant of a broad range of conditions. In summer, it has yellow, bell-shaped flowers atop the cactus.

RATTAIL CACTUS (*Aporocactus flagelliformis*) Rattail cacti have long (up to 6 feet), round stems covered with delicate spines. It is grown for its spectacular fuchsia-pink flowers that may last up to two months and bloom along the length of the stems. This plant is best displayed in a hanging basket.

OLD MAN CACTUS (*Cephalocereus senilis*) This plant is covered with long white hairs, making it resemble an old man who hasn't had a haircut in years. Under these soft-looking hairs are small, sharp spines. It grows slowly, and its nocturnal flowers seldom appear on a plant which is grown indoors.

PINCUSHION CACTUS (*Mammillaria*) Perhaps the most common cactus for growing in the house, these have a wide range of colors and textures. It remains small but may take the form of a single little ball or many balls in clumps. This plant will flower indoors. Flowers appear on top of the plant. It is covered with delicate spines with hooked ends that don't pull out of the skin easily.

BUNNY EARS, PRICKLY PEAR (*Opuntia microdasys*) Bunny ears are some of the most common cactus and will grow outdoors in much of the United States. The broad pads are patterned with small, velvety-looking glochids (a type of spine) that stick in the skin or clothes. It is very low maintenance and, once established, need very little attention. Usually will not bloom when grown indoors.

Old man cactus

Rattail cactus

Bunny ears or prickly pear cactus

Barrel cactus

CHLOROPHYTUM COMOSUM

Spider Plant

Liliaceae

Spider plant hails from South Africa, where it has evolved roots that store water. It tolerates hot, dry conditions, making it an ideal houseplant. It has long, straplike leaves in solid green, green with white edges, white with green edges, and edged in yellow. Spider plant is well-known for its spider "babies," the small plantlets formed at the ends of long stems.

MOISTURE: Allow the soil of spider plant to dry out between waterings.

LIGHT: Provide medium light for spider plant.

TEMPERATURE: Average to somewhat cool temperatures are best. It tolerates hotter temperatures in many cases.

FERTILIZATION: Fertilize only three times in summer using 10-10-10.

PESTS: Watch for mites and scales.

REPOTTING: Repotting is necessary fairly frequently because the thick roots fill a pot quickly. Use an average, well-drained mix.

PROPAGATION: Seed or plantlets.

TIPS: A mass of plantlets indicates the need for repotting (you can propagate them). Spider plant tends to develop brown leaf tips quickly when water stressed. The most effective display is in a hanging basket.

'Vittatum' spider plant

CISSUS RHOMBIFOLIA

Grape Ivy

Vitaceae

Grape ivy has been a favorite houseplant for hundreds of years because it is so easy to grow and lends a lush, tropical look to any room. It is a vining plant with hairy, dark green leaves. Grape ivy is native to Venezuela, so it tolerates high temperatures.

MOISTURE: Let the soil dry out between soakings. Medium humidity keeps the plant looking good.

LIGHT: Provide medium light if possible. Grape ivy tolerates a low-light situation if the plant is grown fairly dry.

TEMPERATURE: Average to hot temperatures produce the best-looking plant.

FERTILIZATION: Fertilize only three times in summer using 10-10-10.

PESTS: Powdery mildew, whiteflies, root rot (can be avoided if soil is allowed to dry slightly between waterings).

REPOTTING: Grape ivy has a minimal root system so seldom needs repotting. Pot when the plant obviously cannot take up any water. Use an average, well-drained potting mix.

Grape ivy

PROPAGATION: Stem cutting is usually the only way to successfully propagate grape ivy. Plants become woody with time, so propagate regularly to have healthy, young plants.

TIPS: Pinch regularly to keep it full and bushy. This plant looks best when grown in a hanging basket, set on a pedestal, or trained on a topiary form. Grape ivy also makes a very attractive ground-cover plant for a large upright specimen such as a weeping fig or a Norfolk Island pine.

Citrus

Citrus plants are impossible to resist, especially in the dead of winter when their waxy, white blossoms fill the room with scent. Citrus houseplants are dwarf types that grow 3 to 4 feet high and have dark, glossy leaves. Most are native to southeast Asia. Choose named cultivars for the best fruiting.

MOISTURE: Keep citrus plants evenly moist at all times.

LIGHT: Bright sun, as high light as possible.

TEMPERATURE: Cool to medium (10° F drop in night temperature).

FERTILIZATION: Citrus are heavy feeders. Use a full-strength acid fertilizer three times in summer or use a dilute-strength fertilizer at every watering using 10-10-30.

PESTS: Whiteflies, aphids, mites and scale insects.

REPOTTING: Seldom need repotting. If you do repot, use a medium weight, well-drained potting mix.

PROPAGATION: Seed or stem cuttings.

'Meyer' lemon

Citrus, lacking natural pollinators, will need to be hand pollinated to bear fruit.

Calamondin orange

TIPS: Prune citrus only to direct growth. Do, however, prune out multiple fruits on large-fruited types. If you grow a citrus tree from seed you will not get the same variety. Nick the seed coat before planting.

TYPES OF CITRUS

LEMON (*Citrus limon*) Meyer lemon and Ponderosa lemon are two of the most popular lemon trees available. They produce full-size lemons, and multiple fruits must be pruned to avoid breaking branches. Both trees grow to about four feet.

CALAMONDIN ORANGE (*Citrofortunella microcarpa*) Calamondin oranges are borne in profusion throughout the year, which means that the plant has small, fragrant flowers, green fruit and ripe fruit on the plant at the same time; a beautiful accent plant.

CLIVIA MINIATA

Clivia

Amaryllidaceae

Clivia

Clivia is well known for bright clusters of yellow, orange, or red flowers, which are followed by red berries. The flower stalks emerge from strappy, bright green leaves that look much like those of an ornamental onion. Clivia originated in South Africa.

MOISTURE: Keep the soil evenly moist in spring and summer. Reduce watering in fall and keep almost dry through the winter rest period. Resume watering when flower stalks appear in early spring.

LIGHT: Provide morning or afternoon direct sun if possible. Avoid noon sun as it can scorch the leaves.

TEMPERATURE: Medium temperature is best when the plant is in active growth, but it must have temperatures below 50° F during the winter rest period. Too warm temperatures may force the plant to flower when it's not ready, which will result in very short flower stalks and quickly fading flowers.

FERTILIZATION: Fertilize with a dilute solution of 10-30-10 every two weeks during active growth. Stop fertilization a month before the rest period begins.

PESTS: Watch for whiteflies and mealybugs.

REPOTTING: Repot every three or four years when the roots have completely filled the pot. Clivia blooms best when pot-bound. Use an average potting mix and a heavy pot since it tends to become top heavy.

PROPAGATION: Propagate by offsets or by division.

TIPS: Remove the individual flowers as soon as they fade so the plant does not produce fruit. The fruit saps energy from the plant, and it may not bloom the following year if they are allowed to develop. Keep the offsets attached to the mother plant for an attractive cluster of blooming plants. Once you've found the right spot for clivia, be sure not to move the plant while it is blooming or it may abort its flowers. Clivia is a most attractive plant even when not in bloom if you regularly groom the foliage.

CODIAEUM VARIEGATUM VAR. PICTUM

Croton

Euphorbiaceae

Croton is a highly valued houseplant because of its brilliantly hued leaves in shades of red, yellow, and green. The leaves are generally leathery and stiff, and borne on bumpy stems. The vary in shape, size, and variegation, depending on the cultivar. Some cultivars even have corkscrew-shape leaves. The plants can grow to about 3 feet tall.

Native to the Malay Peninsula and Pacific Islands, crotons tolerate hot temperatures and high humidity.

MOISTURE: Keep the soil evenly moist and set the plant on a tray of moist pebbles to raise the humidity.

LIGHT: Croton does best in high light. It needs to receive light from the soil level to the top of the plant in order to maintain its bottom leaves and brilliant coloration.

TEMPERATURE: Provide medium to warm temperatures.

FERTILIZATION: Fertilize three times in summer using 10-10-10.

PESTS: Mealybugs, spider mites, and scales. Remove the flowers immediately when they form to avoid attracting insects.

REPOTTING: Repotting is seldom necessary. Pot in an average, well-drained potting mix.

PROPAGATION: Stem cutting, air layering.

TIPS: Croton leaves are easily damaged, so keep plants away from areas where people could brush against them. Plants benefit from spending the summer outside. Plants don't often need pruning but you can cut them back severely if necessary. The sap stains, so be cautious when pruning.

Croton

COLUMNEA

Goldfish Plant

Gesneriaceae

Goldfish plant, a relative of African violet, is grown for its brilliantly colored flowers. The leaves are distinctly tidy and arranged along long, gracefully drooping stems. Native to the tropics, goldfish plant usually grows as an epiphyte. Give it very well drained soil and plenty of humidity and you will benefit from the explosion of red or yellow hooded flowers all along the stems.

MOISTURE: Keep the soil evenly moist while the plant is in active growth, especially while flowering. As with African violets, avoid getting water on the leaves to prevent spotting. Tepid water is best. You'll need to raise humidity levels to help force the plant into bloom.

LIGHT: Provide medium light.

TEMPERATURE: Average temperatures are best.

FERTILIZATION: Fertilize three times in summer or every two weeks with a dilute solution using 10-30-10.

PESTS: Watch for mealybugs.

REPOTTING: Repot annually in a rich mix (one that is full of organic material to hold moisture) for flowering plants.

PROPAGATION: Stem cuttings.

TIPS: It takes skill to get goldfish plant to bloom. If yours won't bloom, try subtly adjusting each element of its culture until you find the right mix.

Goldfish plant

CRASSULA ARGENTEA

Jade Plant

Crassulaceae

Jade plant is one of the most familiar houseplants, particularly because it is so rewarding to grow. This native of South Africa has thick, succulent, glossy green leaves tinged with red on substantial stems. Jade is a long-lived plant that can become quite large. If you have exactly the right conditions, you may get your jade to bloom with pinkish, delicate flowers.

MOISTURE: Allow the soil to dry thoroughly between waterings. Some gardeners water their jades only when the leaves begin to lose their shine or begin to pucker. Although this is a reliable sign that the plant needs water, it stresses the plant and is often followed by leaf drop. However, jade is most often killed by overwatering or poorly drained soil. An overwatered jade will take on a weeping form.

Jade plant

LIGHT: Bright, direct light is best.

TEMPERATURE: Jade tolerates cool to hot temperatures.

FERTILIZATION: Fertilize three times in summer only. 10-10-10.

PESTS: Mealybugs, scales, stem rot.

REPOTTING: Always pot jade in a clay pot, not only for good air movement through the soil, but also for weight. Use a mix for cactus or a well-drained, average potting soil. Repotting is seldom necessary because of the small root system.

PROPAGATION: Jade branches send out aerial roots, and they may also bend and root where they touch the soil. Simply cut off the branch and plant it. Jade can also be easily started by leaf cuttings.

TIPS: Prune your jade as necessary to keep it fairly symmetrical. If it gets one-sided, it may topple because the top of the plant is so heavy. Jade plants naturally have leaves along the thick stems. Some gardeners pinch these leaves off, leaving only leaves at the tops of the branches. This gives the plant an open, architectural look. Rooting new plants all around the base of a plant creates the look of a shrubby thicket.

CYPERUS ISOCLADUS

Dwarf Papyrus

Cyperaceae

Dwarf papyrus is a true sedge with triangular stems and a love of boggy soil. The plant has some leaves at the base, but the most interesting feature is the tuft of bracts at the tops of the 2-foot-tall stems. From these leafy bracts emerge clusters of thin, wiry stems that hold seeds. If you satisfy the few conditions that it prefers, this can be a very low-maintenance plant. Dwarf papyrus is native to South Africa, where it grows along stream banks and in low, waterlogged spots. It is related to the much larger plant used by the ancient Egyptians to make the writing material known as papyrus.

MOISTURE: Keep the soil moist. You can place the pot in a deep saucer of water, keep it filled, and let the plant draw water as it needs it. Do not, however, let the stems become submerged in the water or they will rot. Keep the humidity high or the plant will suffer tip browning.

Dwarf papyrus

LIGHT: High light is preferable.

TEMPERATURE: Average to hot temperatures give the best growth.

FERTILIZATION: Fertilize only once a year using 10-10-10.

PESTS: Watch for stem rot.

REPOTTING: Repot when the rhizomes begin to come out of the pot, preferably in winter or early spring. Use a moisture-retentive soil.

PROPAGATION: Leaf cutting or rhizome division. To propagate by leaf cutting, cut off a leaf and place, upside down, with the stem pointing up, in a pot of water. New leaves will soon appear in the center of the old leaf. During this process, change the water frequently to keep it fresh.

TIPS: Dwarf papyrus is chlorine-sensitive, so let municipally treated water sit exposed to air for 24 hours before watering the plant. This will allow most of the chlorine to evaporate off. Prune dwarf papyrus only as needed to keep it looking good. If your plant is losing and not replacing stems, it is not getting enough light. An attractive way to grow dwarf papyrus is in a clear bowl or container filled with pebbles. Plant the papyrus appropriately and fill the container with water. Keep the water away from the stems and give it bright light, and you have the perfect plant to leave alone while you go on vacation.

DIEFFENBACHIA MACULATA

Spotted Dumb Cane

Araceae

Spotted dumb cane is used extensively in the indoor landscaping industry because it is easy to grow and keep healthy. Native to Central America and northern South America, it has large, pointed leaves that are strikingly variegated with irregular creamy white markings. The plant sends up thick canes from which the leaves unfurl, making the plant a striking architectural addition to the home decor.

MOISTURE: Allow the top inch of soil to dry out between waterings. Provide medium to high humidity.

LIGHT: Medium light. Too little light causes the plant to lose its lower leaves.

TEMPERATURE: Average temperatures are best. Keep the plant out of cold drafts.

FERTILIZATION: Fertilize three times in summer using 10-10-10.

PESTS: Mealybugs and spider mites can sometimes be problems, especially when the humidity is low.

REPOTTING: Repot annually in spring as needed. Use an average, well-drained soil.

PROPAGATION: Air layering, tip cuttings, stem cuttings.

TIPS: The sap from dumb cane can be irritating to the skin and may stain clothing. It is also toxic and may cause swallowing or speaking difficulty, which is where it gets its common name. Be sure to keep it away from children and animals. Prune out old canes occasionally to stimulate new growth. Its leaves are fairly brittle, so place the plant out of the way of foot traffic.

Spotted dumb cane

DIZYGOTHECA ELEGANTISSIMA

False Aralia

Araliaceae

False aralia is one of the most graceful houseplants you can add to your collection. The multiple stems support delicately suspended leaves, giving the plant an elegant appearance. The long, thin leaflets of the compound leaves (one leaf looks like several leaves) are notched, and the tips of the notches are copper colored. The dark, glossy green leaves look almost black in many situations. The petioles (stalks of leaves) and young stems are speckled with white, a distinct contrast to the leaves. Native to Polynesia, this plant thrives with good sunlight and steady moisture.

MOISTURE: Keep the soil evenly moist. Allowing the plant to dry out, even slightly, causes leaf drop. Use a pebble tray to raise the humidity.

False aralia

LIGHT: Medium to bright, filtered light.

TEMPERATURE: Average to warm temperatures.

FERTILIZATION: Fertilize three times in summer using 10-10-10.

PESTS: Mealybugs, scales, spider mites. Lower leaves may drop when plants are exposed to drafts.

REPOTTING: Repot only occasionally and use a well-drained, moisture-retentive soil.

PROPAGATION: Air layering or stem cuttings.

TIPS: As the plant matures, the false aralia's leaf shape may change. To maintain the look of the young leaves, prune the plant back substantially. For a full, shrubby-looking plant, pot several false aralias of different sizes in one container. When you find a location where the plant thrives, leave it there. Plants lose lower leaves as they grow older.

Dracaena

Agavaceae

The wide variety of dracaenas available has made them extremely popular. The large, easy-to-care-for plants are as architecturally imposing as pieces of furniture. Their origin in tropical Africa makes them humidity lovers.

MOISTURE: Allow the top inch of soil to dry between waterings. Add humidity with a pebble tray to prevent tip browning.

LIGHT: Low to medium light.

TEMPERATURE: Average temperatures

FERTILIZATION: Fertilize only once a year unless you want to force growth using 10-10-10.

PESTS: Mealybugs and spider mites may be problems.

REPOTTING: Repot only as needed to give the roots more room. This will vary according to species.

PROPAGATION: Air layering or stem cutting.

TIPS: Prune only for grooming.

TYPES OF DRACAENA

'JANET CRAIG' (*Dracaena deremensis*) This dracaena is the smallest type, although it does eventually grow to about 4 feet tall. It has long, dark, glossy leaves that are held close to the stems. Although the species has solid green leaves, several cultivars with lighter green leaves striped with white are available.

MASS CANE (*Dracaena fragrans*) Mass cane is the most commonly available dracaena. It's often called corn plant because of its long, straplike leaves. The cultivar called 'Massangeana' has leaves striped with yellow. Usually, leafy mass cane stems are planted in one pot. Plants tend to lose lower leaves and can look sparse after a few years.

'Warneckii' striped dracaena

Madagascar dragontree

MADAGASCAR DRAGONTREE (*Dracaena marginata*) This plant is a unique architectural accent. Its slender stems meander this way and that, ending in tufts of lancelike leaves of green and maroon. It can grow to 8 feet tall. The plant tends to lose its lower leaves as it grows, but because of the distinctive look of the stems, it doesn't seem to matter aesthetically. The cultivar 'Tricolor' has leaves with shades of white, pink, and green.

SONG OF INDIA (*Dracaena reflexa* or *pleomele*) With many small leaves tightly hugging the wandering stems, this is a very tropical-looking plant. The stems can become so heavy with leaves that they need to be supported. The most common variety is 'Variegata', with yellow-edged leaves; it needs medium light to keep its variegation.

'Variegata' variegated song of India

Song of India

EPIPREMNUM AUREUM

Pothos or Devil's Ivy

Araceae

Native to Southeast Asia, pothos is a vining plant widely used in hanging baskets or trained on moss stakes. Its heart-shaped leaves are shiny green and marked with irregular yellow variegation. Pothos takes neglect, low light, and poor watering practices with ease.
MOISTURE: Allow the soil to dry to 2 inches below the surface between waterings.
LIGHT: Provide bright filtered light if possible. The plant will do just fine in lower light, but the variegation may be lost.
TEMPERATURE: Average temperatures are best during the active growth period.

FERTILIZATION: Fertilize three times in summer, using 10-10-10, if you want growth. Otherwise, no need to fertilize.
PESTS: Mealybugs and scales, but generally problem free.
REPOTTING: Repot only when needed as the roots fill the pot. By moving it into a larger pot each spring, you will encourage new growth.
PROPAGATION: Pothos roots easily from stem cuttings or layering. Cuttings can be rooted in water or soil.
TIPS: Give it a winter rest (reduce watering and lower temperature to around 60° F). Prune stems just above a node to reduce the plant's size. Regularly start new plants to have a fresh plant to replace a tired one.

Pothos

EUPHORBIA MILII

Crown-of-Thorns

Euphorbiaceae

This plant from Madagascar can virtually bloom year-round in good light. Long, spoon-shape leaves appear at the ends of the branches, and clusters of tiny flowers appear on stalks at the ends of the branches. The flowers are tiny and are surrounded by a pair of bright red, yellow, or salmon bracts. Each stem is covered with small, sharp spines.
MOISTURE: Allow the top inch or so of soil to dry out when the plant is blooming. When the plant is not in bloom, let about half the soil ball dry from the surface. Don't let the

entire soil ball dry out, however, or it will drop its leaves. Keep the humidity low.
LIGHT: Direct sun produces the best bloom, but it can tolerate average light.
TEMPERATURE: Average to hot.
FERTILIZATION: Fertilize three times in summer using 10-30-10.
PESTS: Mealybugs and stem rot.
REPOTTING: Repot infrequently and use average potting soil or a soil mix designed for cactus.
PROPAGATION: Propagate by stem cuttings or division.
TIPS: All euphorbias have an irritating sap. Be sure to wash your hands thoroughly after handling. If your plant dries out and loses its leaves, it will grow new ones after you begin watering; however, you will have a bare plant for a few weeks.

Crown-of-thorns

FATSIA JAPONICA

Japanese Fatsia

Araliaceae

Japanese fatsia, a native of Japan, is another of the most tolerant houseplants, especially when it comes to temperature. It is shrubby, up to 6 feet high. Its large, bold, tropical leaves are coarse textured. There is a bright yellow, variegated cultivar available.
MOISTURE: Let soil dry very slightly between waterings. Give it a winter rest period by reducing watering. If it dries out completely, it will lose its lower leaves.
LIGHT: Medium light. It tolerates low light although it may become stretched and thin.
TEMPERATURE: Cool best but higher temperatures are tolerated for short periods.

FERTILIZATION: Fertilize three times in summer using 10-10-10.
PESTS: Mealybugs, scales, aphids, or mites.
REPOTTING: Repot annually until maximum size is reached. Then, pot only when the plant seems to be overwhelming its pot. Fatsias are top heavy because of the size of the leaves, so use a heavy, stable pot and a rich, well-drained potting mix.
PROPAGATION: Stem cuttings.
TIPS: A beautiful accent plant for a large, wide-open area. One of the few plants that will tolerate growing near a sliding glass door or other doorway. Fatsia seldom needs pruning except for grooming, but you can prune hard to regulate its size.

Japanese fatsia

Ferns

Maidenhair fern

Ferns range from the feathery fronds of the common Boston fern to the flat, odd-shaped leaves of the staghorn fern. Some are terrestrial, and others are epiphytes, which derive their water and nutrients from the air and rain.

MOISTURE: Keep soil moist and provide plenty of humidity.

LIGHT: Medium to bright filtered light. Full sun can damage the fronds, and they don't perform well in homes with low light.

TEMPERATURE: Average-to-warm temperatures.

FERTILIZATION: Fertilize ferns three times in summer or with a dilute solution at every watering to force growth using 10-10-10.

PESTS: Scales, spider mites, and mealybugs.

REPOTTING: Repot when the roots begin to push out of the pot. Use a rich soil for terrestrial types and a coarse mix for epiphytes.

PROPAGATION: By dividing rhizomes or by spores.

TIPS: Ferns reproduce by spores on the back sides of the leaves. The spore cases resemble scales, but are in a regular pattern.

Bird's-nest fern

TYPES OF FERNS

MAIDENHAIR FERN (*Adiantum* species) Maidenhair ferns all have thin, hairlike stems. All types have a delicate, fine texture and do best if allowed to slightly dry out between waterings.

BIRD'S-NEST FERN (*Asplenium nidus*) Bird's-nest fern, native to tropical Asia, has wide, straplike leaves of light green. An epiphyte, it must have a very coarse soil. Keep the soil moisture even, or the tips will die back.

SWORD FERN (*Nephrolepis* species) Perhaps the best known of all the ferns, this group includes Boston fern. All types have long fronds with many leaflets. These are terrestrial ferns, which need a rich, moisture-retentive potting mix.

STAGHORN FERN (*Platycerium bifurcatum*) The large, gray-green fronds look much like deer antlers and are a favorite of collectors. It can be grown on a slab of bark, attached to a wad of sphagnum moss. When grown in this manner, they must be watered almost every day.

RABBIT'S-FOOT FERN (*Polypodium aureum*) With long fronds and thick, furry rhizomes (from which it gets its name) that sometimes creep over the edge of the pot, this fern needs constant moisture. The wavy, long fronds are borne on long, slender stalks and the undersides are covered with golden brown spore cases.

Rabbit's-foot fern

*'Bostoniensis'
Boston fern*

Staghorn fern

Ficus, Fig

Moraceae

Figs are native to tropical and subtropical regions all over the world. They vary from large trees to minute ground covers, with all manner of leaf shapes and colors. All have a milky sap that stains, and some of them are used commercially for their edible fruit.

MOISTURE: Allow the soil to dry out slightly between waterings. Average humidity; only a few need high humidity.

LIGHT: All levels of light. But changing it can cause leaf drop.

TEMPERATURE: Average temperatures are best. Do not change once established.

FERTILIZATION: Fertilize three times in summer for growth; once a year will keep the plant within bounds. Use 10-10-10.

PESTS: Scales are a major problem on the tree forms; mealybugs and mites may be problems.

REPOTTING: Smaller varieties do best if repotted annually into a slightly larger pot. Larger specimens can stay in the same pot by changing the soil and pruning roots. Use a rich, moisture-retentive potting mix.

PROPAGATION: Trailing types by stem cutting; larger types by seed or air layering.

TIPS: Prune to keep the plants looking good and in the right form.

TYPES OF FICUS

WEEPING FIG (*Ficus benjamina*) Weeping fig is one of the most beloved houseplants and will grow large under even average conditions. Its weeping form is easy to maintain with occasional pruning. It can be kept at 6 feet or allowed to grow to 20 feet. Very sensitive to change, it will shed leaves at the slightest provocation.

Weeping fig

INDIA RUBBER TREE (*Ficus elastica*) The rubber tree takes almost no maintenance except dusting of its large leaves. It grows in a single stem unless pruned. When pruning, dust the cut with powdered charcoal.

FIDDLE-LEAF FIG (*Ficus lyrata*) Fiddle-leaf fig grows quite large and demands a large site. The dark green leaves are pale underneath and have an undulating shape, from which the plant gets it common name. Fiddle-leaf fig may also be pruned to control its size.

CREEPING FIG (*Ficus pumila*) This plant enhances a hanging basket or makes a superb topiary when grown on a form filled with sphagnum moss. It grows well in low light and makes an excellent ground cover for large pots.

Fiddle-leaf fig

India rubber tree

Creeping fig

FITTONIA VERSCHAFFELTII

Nerve Plant

Acanthaceae

Nerve plants hail from the rain forests of South and Central America. They are small, ground-hugging plants that make a beautiful addition to dish gardens and terrariums. Their small leaves are borne on thin stems, and the distinctions that make it so popular are the intricate veining on the leaves and the color of the stems. Some are red to pink; others are silver.

MOISTURE: Keep the soil evenly moist but not soaked, and provide as much humidity as you can to mimic rain-forest conditions.

LIGHT: Nerve plant survives well in medium light and should be kept out of direct sun, which can damage its leaves. Bright light in winter helps keep the plant in the best condition.

Nerve plant

TEMPERATURE: Warm to average temperatures are best, although it tolerates cooler temperatures occasionally.

FERTILIZATION: Fertilize monthly to keep plants actively growing, using 10-10-10.

PESTS: Usually pest free, but keep an eye out for mealybugs and spider mites, especially if not grown in ideal conditions.

REPOTTING: Pot in a very rich, moisture-retentive soil. It is not a fast grower so seldom needs repotting except when starting new plants. It seldom needs a larger pot than what you start with.

PROPAGATION: Propagate by stem cuttings or layering. Old plants often lose their attractiveness, so take regular stem or tip cuttings to produce new plants.

TIPS: Nerve plant should be pinched regularly to keep the plant full and bushy. It makes excellent ground cover under larger plants in large pots as long as its growing needs are met. It will trail over the edges of a container. Several cultivars are available, some with silver veins and some in miniature form. If you place a fittonia in a wide pot, the tips will naturally take root. You can detach these from the mother plant or keep the new plants to grow as a cluster. In spring, cut back hard to produce new, bushy growth.

HEDERA

Ivy

Araliaceae

If there exists a perfectly adaptable plant that thrives in almost any condition, it must be ivy. Often called English ivy as a group, these plants from Europe and northern Africa are easy to grow and come in an infinite number of shapes and colors. The plant has trailing woody stems and vary from the typical three-lobed English ivy to leaves in yellow, gold, white, silver, and pink.

MOISTURE: Allow the top inch of soil to dry out between waterings. Needs a winter rest period in which you water sparingly. If grown in warm temperatures, give it plenty of humidity.

LIGHT: Bright light if possible. Variegated types look best if given some sunlight every day. In low light it looks spindly.

TEMPERATURE: English ivy grows best in cool temperatures, although it tolerates some warmth. Does best if given a rest

Algerian ivy

'Shamrock' English ivy

period in winter with temperatures at about 50° F.

FERTILIZATION: Use a dilute solution of 10-10-10 at each watering during active growth. None during rest period.

PESTS: Scales can be a serious problem; control with horticultural oil. Watch for spider mites in dry locations and spray leaves frequently with a strong water spray to keep them at bay. Insecticidal soap controls them.

REPOTTING: Pot in a rich, moisture-retentive soil. Ivy seldom needs repotting.

PROPAGATION: Stem and tip cuttings and by layering.

TIPS: English ivy has aerial roots and can grow on a wooden trellis or a moss pole. It tolerates pruning well, and its trailing stems make it a perfect candidate for growing on a topiary frame. In hanging baskets several plants may be grouped for a thick, bushy display. Pinch out the tips to keep the plants looking full.

ALGERIAN IVY (*Hedera canariensis*) Algerian ivy has the largest leaves and is the most vigorous of the ivies. The leaves are deep green with maroon petioles. Unlike most ivies, it doesn't branch when pinched. Should be grown in a hanging basket or as a ground cover under large plants to use it to best advantage.

HIBISCUS ROSA-SINENSIS

Chinese Hibiscus

Malvaceae

Native to tropical Asia, hibiscus is one of the most sought-after houseplants because of its intensely colored, tropical flowers. It lends an exotic air to any room. Its glossy, dark green lobed leaves are the perfect foil to the 5- to 6-inch flowers in all shades of red, coral, yellow, pink, brown, blue, and white. The prominent stamens add to the floral display.

Hundreds of cultivars are available with all shapes of leaves, some variegated types, and all types of flowers, including doubles.

MOISTURE: Always keep evenly moist during the growth period and water just enough to keep the soil from drying out during its winter rest. The plant performs well with a pebble humidity tray.

LIGHT: Provide very high light. Direct sun for several hours a day is desirable.

TEMPERATURE: Average temperatures will give the best results during the growth period; provide cooler temperatures during its rest.

FERTILIZATION: Fertilize with a dilute solution of 10-30-10 at every watering during the growth period.

PESTS: Scales, whiteflies, mealybugs, spider mites, and aphids can present problems to the plant.

REPOTTING: Hibiscus seldom needs repotting unless you wish to force new growth or the roots grow out the bottom of the pot. Use a mix for flowering plants.

PROPAGATION: Propagate Chinese hibiscus by tip cuttings.

TIPS: Hibiscus flowers on new wood, so don't prune it off or you will lose the flower buds. To keep the plant shrubby and attractive, prune it back hard in late winter. Root-prune in the same ratio and repot in fresh soil at the same time.

This technique induces new growth with plenty of blooms in spring. Hibiscus will drop its leaves if conditions change, but the plant quickly regenerates its leaves on old stems. Remove all spent flowers and stalks to keep the plant tidy and neat.

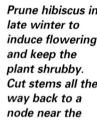

Chinese hibiscus

Prune hibiscus in late winter to induce flowering and keep the plant shrubby. Cut stems all the way back to a node near the crown.

HOYA CARNOSA

Wax Plant

Asclepiadaceae

Hoya, native to South China and Australia, is a perfect candidate for a hanging basket with long vines of waxy, succulent foliage tipped with clusters of striking flowers that resemble milkweed blossoms. Although the species has long, narrow, shiny green leaves, there are cultivars with curly or crinkly leaves as well as variegated types with leaves of pink and white. The flowers are white to pale pink with a red center, and are elegantly fragrant at night. The plant is sometimes called honey plant because the flowers exude a fragrant, honeylike nectar.

MOISTURE: Allow the top ½ inch of soil to dry between waterings during the plant's growth period. Don't let it dry out completely though during its winter rest. Humidity encourages flowers.

LIGHT: Provide medium to bright light. Direct sun encourages flowering.

TEMPERATURE: Hoya does best in average to warm temperatures. Avoid cold drafts.

FERTILIZATION: Fertilize three times in summer using 10-30-10.

PESTS: Scales, mealybugs; be particularly careful of insect pests when the plant is blooming.

REPOTTING: Repot infrequently. Hoya has a minimal root system, and repotting is always a great shock. Pot in an average, well-drained mix.

PROPAGATION: Stem cuttings. Set the cuttings in a combination of coarse vermiculite and perlite.

TIPS: Hoya is easily trained onto wire supports, which help to support the thin stems when it is heavy with leaves. Do not remove flower stems after blooming because this is where next season's flowers grow. Prune only as necessary to keep the stems from becoming too heavy. The stems exude a milky sap when cut. Although most often grown as foliage plants, good conditions will help produce the fragrant flowers. Watch for pests; bugs love the honeylike sap.

Wax plant

HYPOESTES PHYLLOSTACHYA

Polka-Dot Plant

Acanthaceae

Polka-dot plant is popular for indoor and outdoor gardens, where its bright pink, speckled leaves add a touch of gaiety. Native to Madagascar, it is a fast grower and can reach 2 feet in the home. Although primarily grown for its foliage, it will produce stalks of tiny purple flowers. Some cultivars have white or red spotted leaves, always on a base of olive green.

MOISTURE: Average moisture, letting the top ½ inch of soil dry out between waterings. After flowering, it goes into a brief dormant period; only water enough to keep the soil from drying out completely.

LIGHT: Medium to bright filtered light. It survives low light, but the markings fade.

TEMPERATURE: Average to warm temperatures are best.

FERTILIZATION: Fertilize three times in summer using 10-30-10.

PESTS: Mealybugs and whiteflies may be a problem.

REPOTTING: Repot annually with an average potting mix or start new plants.

PROPAGATION: This plant becomes old and unattractive fairly quickly, so start over annually from tip cuttings.

TIPS: Pinch polka-dot plant regularly to keep it bushy. After flowering, the plant tends to stretch and become spindly, so cut to the ground and allow to regenerate.

Polka-dot plant

KALANCHOE TOMENTOSA

Panda Plant

Crassulaceae

Panda plant is native to Madagascar, where it has evolved to tolerate dryness and high heat. Unlike its flowering cousin, *Kalanchoe blossfeldiana*, this plant is grown strictly for its foliage. The thick leaves are covered with soft silver hairs, which give the plant a fuzzy, blue-gray appearance. The edges of the leaves are tipped with chocolate brown or rust hairs. The plant grows to about 1½ feet tall, with the leaves borne in rosettes on slender stems.

MOISTURE: Allow the top 2 inches of soil to dry between waterings. During winter, water only enough to keep the plant from drying out.

LIGHT: High light is recommended, with some direct sun.

TEMPERATURE: Panda plant tolerates cool to warm temperatures. It should be given cool temperatures in the winter.

FERTILIZATION: Fertilize three times in summer with 10-30-10.

PESTS: Mealybugs.

REPOTTING: Panda plant needs repotting only infrequently. Pot in an average, well-drained soil.

PROPAGATION: Stem or leaf cuttings.

TIPS: Although it tolerates pruning well, panda plant seldom needs to be pruned except for occasional removal of a wayward stem.

Panda plant

MARANTA LEUCONEURA

Prayer Plant

Marantaceae

Prayer plant, so-called because of its unusual habit of folding its leaves upward at night, is a popular foliage plant because of its coloration. The species has soft green leaves with dark green or brown feathery variegation. A multitude of cultivars is available with leaves marked with silver, pink, maroon, olive, and yellow. The undersides of the leaves are usually maroon. Prayer plant is native to Brazilian rain forests.

MOISTURE: Keep the soil evenly moist and the humidity high to avoid brown edges. Allow the upper half of the soil to dry out during the winter rest period.

LIGHT: Medium light is best. High light, especially direct sun, causes the leaves to dry and brown at the edges.

TEMPERATURE: Average warmth is best for prayer plant, with a drop to about 50° F during the winter.

FERTILIZATION: Fertilize every two weeks with a dilute solution using 10-10-10.

PESTS: Watch out for mealybugs and spider mites.

REPOTTING: Pot in an organic, well-drained soil. Repotting may be necessary in spring.

PROPAGATION: Propagate by stem cuttings or division.

TIPS: Prayer plant is an excellent candidate for a terrarium because of the naturally high humidity. To keep the humidity high, group it with other plants.

Prayer plant

MONSTERA DELICIOSA

Swiss-Cheese Plant (Split-Leaf Philodendron)

Araceae

Swiss-cheese plant, native to the rain forests of Central America, is a distinct, dramatic addition to the indoor garden. In the wild, the plants climb trees, clinging with aerial roots. You can simulate this by providing a moss pole. The plants can grow 10 to 15 feet high and 8 feet across, so they need a large space.

MOISTURE: Allow the top ½ inch of soil to dry out between waterings. Allow to dry more thoroughly in winter. Higher humidity will prevent the leaf tips from browning.

LIGHT: Provide bright, filtered light. Plants in lower light tend to stretch and to produce smaller leaves without holes.

TEMPERATURE: Average. If grown in warm temperatures, it is necessary to increase the humidity.

FERTILIZATION: Fertilize three times in summer using 10-10-10.

PESTS: Mealybugs, aphids.

REPOTTING: Pot in an organic mix. Repot annually until plant is desired size. Then add fresh topdress annually.

PROPAGATION: Tip cuttings.

TIPS: The leaves need to be washed regularly. On a moss pole, train the aerial roots into the moss. Otherwise, train them down into the potting soil.

Swiss-cheese plant

NOLINA RECURVATA (BEAUCARNEA)

Ponytail Palm, Elephant-Foot Tree

Agavaceae

This succulent plant from the southwestern United States and Mexico has adapted to the desert life. Its huge, swollen base stores water, and the long, sometimes curly, straplike leaves have very little leaf surface to lose moisture. It can grow to 6 feet or more and is the perfect plant for the neglectful gardener. It lends a distinct southwestern flair to the interior decor. Mature plants have a swollen base resembling an elephant's foot, the source of their common name.

MOISTURE: Allow the soil to dry almost completely before watering. Keep the humidity low if possible.

LIGHT: High light, but it adapts to medium light. Direct sun is preferable.

TEMPERATURE: Hot is best, but adapts easily to medium temperatures. If grown at a cool temperature, it should be seldom watered.

FERTILIZATION: Fertilize infrequently; once a year using 10-10-10.

PESTS: Mealybugs.

REPOTTING: Pot in a fast-draining mix, such as a cactus mix. Repot infrequently; putting it in a larger pot encourages growth.

PROPAGATION: Ponytail palm is very difficult for the home gardener to propagate.

TIPS: This plant rarely needs pruning except to remove dead leaves at the bottom.

Ponytail palm

OSMANTHUS FRAGRANS

Sweet Olive

Oleaceae

Although not an unusually striking foliage plant, sweet olive is worth growing for the fragrance of its flowers. This shrubby plant has leathery, dark green leaves, which lightly resemble holly leaves, along pale brown stems. Tiny, creamy white flowers emit an orange-blossom scent that fills the room. Leaves are slow to replace themselves, but the plant produces flowers all year long. Native to eastern Asia, this plant is one of the most care-free you will find for the home.

MOISTURE: Allow the top inch of soil to dry between waterings. As a houseplant, it performs best in low humidity.

LIGHT: High light; direct sun increases flower production.

TEMPERATURE: Average to warm. Will grow in cool conditions as well, or in average temperature with a drop in night temperature.

FERTILIZATION: Fertilize three times in summer using 10-30-10.

PESTS: Watch for spider mites if growing in low humidity.

REPOTTING: Pot in an average, well-drained mix. Sweet olive grows very slowly so seldom needs repotting.

PROPAGATION: Tip cuttings.

TIPS: Sweet olive benefits from being put outdoors in a partially shaded location in summer. The plant rarely needs pruning because it grows so slowly. Don't be quick to prune off what looks like dead stem tips. These will bear flowers.

Sweet olive

Palms

Palmae

Palms have long been favored as houseplants not only because of their low-maintenance needs but also because their attractive fronds lend a tropical feel to the home. Their large size makes them superb decorating features. Palm fronds vary according to the species, but they can range from 6 inches to many feet long. Most palms have only one growing point from which the fronds arise.

MOISTURE: Allow the soil to dry briefly between waterings for most species. Some species need to be kept evenly moist.

LIGHT: Medium to filtered bright light is best.

TEMPERATURE: Average, as noted below.

FERTILIZATION: Fertilize three times in summer using 10-10-10.

PESTS: Scales, spider mites, and mealybugs can be problems.

REPOTTING: Average, well-drained potting mix, and repot infrequently.

PROPAGATION: By seed. Because they rarely produce flowers indoors, you will have to rely on a plant supplier for new plants.

TIPS: Allow plenty of room for a palm to spread. They can all be damaged easily, especially the sago palm. Prune only to remove a damaged or old frond.

Fishtail palm

TYPES OF PALMS

SAGO PALM (*Cycas revoluta*) Not a true palm but a cycad, this slow-growing plant has stiff, dark green fronds, and only one or two are borne each year in the center of the plant. More tolerant of low light than the other palms, sago palm benefits from a rest period in winter with little water.

Sago palm

FISHTAIL PALM (*Caryota mitis*) The fishtail palm has delightfully asymmetrical leaves that look irregularly torn at the tips. The plant produces suckers at the base, making it full and shrubby. The arching fronds have leaflets for their entire length, and the fronds can grow up to 8 feet long.

BAMBOO PALM (*Chamaedorea seifrizii erumpens*) Native to Mexico and Central America, this is the fastest growing of all the palms. It remains fairly small and is more tolerant of low light than any of the other true palms.

ARECA PALM (*Chrysalidocarpus lutescens*) Native to Madagascar, areca palm is large and graceful. Light green fronds, about a foot across, emerge from the tips of stems. The fronds can be up to 4 or 5 feet long, and their arching habit makes this a very large plant.

Bamboo palm

KENTIA PALM (*Howea forsterana*) Kentia palm is often seen in hotel lobbies or theater atriums. The long, arching stems give the plant an elegant demeanor. Easy to grow and extremely tolerant, it can grow up to 10 feet tall and wide.

LADY PALM (*Raphis excelsa*) Lady palm tolerates low light very well. It does best in evenly moist soil, unlike many other palms, and is extremely slow growing.

Areca palm

Kentia palm

Lady palm

PEPEROMIA CAPERATA

Peperomia

Piperaceae

Peperomia has been cultivated for so long that its country of origin is in question. This immensely popular houseplant has dark green, heart-shaped, crinkled leaves and succulent red or pink stems. The plant produces creamy flower spikes throughout the year. Although some gardeners grow peperomia purely for its foliage and pinch the flower spikes out, the flowers add an attractive dimension. There is an abundance of cultivars to choose from, with a wide range of colors and textures available.

MOISTURE: Allow to dry slightly between waterings.

Peperomia

Overwatering can quickly cause root rot. Also provide extra humidity in dry rooms.

LIGHT: Grow in medium to low light. Variegated varieties especially will benefit from a few hours a day of filtered bright light.

TEMPERATURE: Average to warm temperatures are best.

FERTILIZATION: Fertilize three times in summer using 10-10-10.

PESTS: Mealybugs appear to be the only pest peperomia has. Subject to root rot if overwatered.

REPOTTING: Repot into a larger pot if it starts in a small one. It has very minimal root systems, so once they are in a 5-inch pot, it will not need repotting. Use an organic, well-drained potting mix.

PROPAGATION: Propagate by tip cuttings or leaf cuttings.

TIPS: Prune only by pinching out leaves that make the plant unattractive because of elongated petioles. If your peperomia plant starts to elongate into a central stem, then it is time to take cuttings and produce a new plant.

Philodendron

Araceae

Philodendrons are among the most adaptable of all houseplants. Their large, shiny leaves add a tropical dimension to rooms. In the wild—in South American rain forests—they are epiphytes and grow as vines, shrubs, or trees. They are strong, sturdy plants, which don't require much light and can tolerate many conditions.

MOISTURE: Allow the soil to dry slightly between waterings. Give them a winter rest—water only enough to keep the potting mix from drying out completely.

LIGHT: Grow in low to medium light.

TEMPERATURE: Provide average temperatures.

FERTILIZATION: Fertilize three times in summer with 10-10-10 if you want the plant to grow. Otherwise, fertilize once a year.

PESTS: Mealybugs.

REPOTTING: Repot only when roots have filled the pot and the plant can no longer take up water. Use an average, well-drained soil mix.

PROPAGATION: Propagate by stem cuttings (either in water or soil).

TIPS: In winter, keep the potting mix on the dry side and keep it from getting cold or the plant will develop root rot.

TYPES OF PHILODENDRONS

TREE PHILODENDRON (*Philodendron selloum*) Tree philodendron, with its deeply cut, shiny green leaves, is a beautiful addition to rooms with lots of space. The plant produces a stem about 6 inches tall and from this emerge large leaves on 2- to 3-foot petioles. If you lack space, place it high on a pedestal to allow the leaves to cascade naturally. Direct aerial roots back into the pot.

PARLOR IVY OR HEART-LEAF PHILODENDRON (*Philodendron scandens*) Parlor ivy has been around for hundreds of years and is still popular because of its ability to look superb even in low light. The climbing stems bear heart-shaped, deep green leaves that are bronze when they begin to unfold. It does well when trained on a moss pole or suspended in a basket. If you pinch regularly, it will stay shrubby and attractive. Dust or shower the leaves often to help keep parlor ivy looking its best.

Tree philodendron

Heart-leaf philodendron

PILEA MICROPHYLLA

Artillery Plant

Urticaceae

Artillery plant is native to the American Tropics and tolerates a range of conditions. Its tiny oval leaves are deeply crinkled, fleshy, and medium to dusty green. The plant has an overall fine, textured look because of the small leaves, which are borne in flat rosettes along sturdy, arching stems. The plant is exceedingly easy to grow and gets its name from the explosive way in which it throws pollen whenever watered. This causes it to become weedy in greenhouses, popping up anywhere there is a bit of soil. Some variegated cultivars are available.

MOISTURE: Allow the top 2 inches of the potting mix to dry between waterings. Water thoroughly but don't let the plant sit with very moist soil. It does like high humidity, however.

LIGHT: Provide medium light. Artillery plant does very poorly in bright light, particularly in sunlight.

TEMPERATURE: Artillery plant tolerates all temperature ranges.

FERTILIZATION: Fertilize infrequently to keep the plant short and shrubby, using 10-10-10.

PESTS: Spider mites, mealybugs, and scales can cause problems.

REPOTTING: Repotting is seldom necessary. By the time the plant has outgrown its pot, it has become fairly unsightly and you may decide to toss it. If not, pot in an average, well-drained potting mix.

PROPAGATION: Tip cuttings root easily.

TIPS: Pinch the plant frequently to keep it shrubby. It is most attractive when young, however, so start new plants regularly so you can replace old ones that have become unsightly. You can pinch pilea regularly to keep it shrubby, but it almost always becomes unsightly eventually. If you make it part of your routine to start new plants often, you'll always have prime specimens to display.

Artillery plant

PLECTRANTHUS AUSTRALIS

Swedish Ivy

Lamiaceae

This fast-growing member of the mint family is native to southeastern Australia. The plant has succulent, square stems that bear waxy, rich green leaves in pairs. The stems drape beautifully from a hanging basket and can reach several feet if not pinched back. A well-grown plant will produce stems of soft pink flowers that are borne above the foliage. As do other members of the mint family, Swedish ivy produces a scent when the leaves are bruised or the stems are pinched. The stems will take root wherever a node touches the soil.

MOISTURE: Swedish ivy performs best if the soil is kept evenly moist. Although it will tolerate drier conditions, long periods of dryness will cause the plant to produce smaller and smaller leaves.

LIGHT: Medium light will produce the most attractive plant.

TEMPERATURE: Average temperatures are best, but the plant tolerates cool temperatures as well.

FERTILIZATION: Fertilize three times in summer or with a dilute solution at every watering using 10-10-10. If the plant begins to produce smaller and smaller leaves, check your watering, and if that is satisfactory, fertilize the plant more often. If the plant doesn't respond after this, it probably is old and is giving you a hint that it's time to start a new one.

PESTS: Mealybugs and whiteflies may cause problems for Swedish ivy.

REPOTTING: Repotting is seldom necessary. By the time a plant has outgrown its pot, it usually looks unattractive and is best discarded. If you regularly start new plants from tip cuttings, you will always have attractive plants. Use a potting mix high in organic material.

PROPAGATION: Tip cuttings root readily in water or soil.

TIPS: Swedish ivy is beautiful when grown in a hanging basket, and it can make an attractive topiary grown on a wire frame. Pinch the tips regularly to keep the plant shrubby (you may want to use pruners because the sap will turn your fingers orange).

P. purpuratus, purple Swedish ivy, has the same general attributes as *P. australis* except that the leaves and stems are a delicious purple color.

Swedish ivy

Purple
Swedish ivy

POLYSCIAS BALFOURIANA

Balfour Aralia

Araliaceae

Native to New Caledonia in the southwest Pacific, balfour aralia is a strikingly elegant small tree for the home interior. The plant grows to about 3 feet high. The medium green leaves are round with deeply serrated margins, and cultivars are available with subtle cream variegation on the edges of the leaves. As a plant ages, the leaves may become compound, composed of several round leaflets. *P. fruticosa*, ming aralia, has finely dissected leaves, reminiscent of a fern, and can grow larger. This aralia will tolerate lower light than balfour aralia.

MOISTURE: Allow the top inch of soil to dry out between waterings. Allow the plant a winter rest by reducing water. High humidity is important to keep the plant in top form—pebble trays work well.

LIGHT: Provide medium to bright filtered light but no direct sun.

TEMPERATURE: Balfour aralia is sensitive to temperature and must be kept warm (65° F or more), and so must the soil.

FERTILIZATION: Fertilize with a dilute solution at every watering (fertilizing three times a year can be too much of a shock for this plant) using 10-10-10.

PESTS: Balfour aralia often has problems with spider mites and scales. Higher humidity should keep the mites at bay.

REPOTTING: Repotting is seldom necessary. Pot in an average, well-drained potting mix.

PROPAGATION: Reproduce by tip cuttings. Use a rooting hormone, keep the cutting warm, and be patient. Balfour aralia can also be propagated by air layering.

TIPS: Balfour aralia can be very sensitive to change and will often drop many leaves as it adjusts to new conditions. A new plant may need several weeks of adjustment before it ceases leaf drop. Again, be patient and continue to subtly adjust your culture until you have it right. When you do, try to avoid moving the plant or changing the culture unnecessarily. Prune frequently to keep in good form.

'Marginata' balfour aralia

RADERMACHERA SINICA

China Doll

Bignoniaceae

Native to China, the China doll has only recently become a widely available houseplant. Although its compound leaves are actually quite large, the leaflets are small and graceful, giving the plant a delicate, fernlike appearance. The leaves are rich glossy green, with deeply veined, pointed leaflets, and grow from woody stems. Many can be planted together in one pot, for a fuller look.

MOISTURE: Keep the soil moist at all times. The plant tolerates low humidity.

LIGHT: Bright filtered to medium light will keep the plant at its most attractive.

TEMPERATURE: Average temperatures are fine, but the winter temperature should not be allowed to drop below 50° F.

FERTILIZATION: Fertilize three times during summer using 10-10-10.

PESTS: Keep an eye out for mealybugs and spider mites, especially if the plant is grown in low humidity.

REPOTTING: Pot in a rich, moisture-retentive soil. Repotting for China doll is seldom needed.

PROPAGATION: Propagate by stem cuttings.

TIPS: Until recently, China doll has not been readily available in the greenhouse industry. If you are fortunate enough to acquire one, you may be the first among your friends to have one, which makes it hard to know how to treat it. Prune only as needed to keep the plant somewhat symmetrical and to remove dead leaves. China doll is a perfect plant to put on a pedestal for the look of a small tree without taking up too much room. Shower the plant regularly to keep the leaves at their best. Pinch to encourage bushiness. In nature it can become quite sprawling.

China doll

SAINTPAULIA

African Violet

Gesneriaceae

The African violet is one of the most frequently hybridized and displayed houseplants. Although primarily grown for its beautiful flowers, the foliage is lovely in itself. The leaves grow in rosettes, with stout petioles bearing round to oval, softly fuzzy leaves. The leaves usually have a smooth edge, but some are serrated, undulating, or crinkled. Some varieties have variegated leaves. Plants range from a couple of inches across to as large as 1½ feet wide. The single or double flowers, usually about an inch across, are borne in large clusters and come in all colors, including bicolors and picotees, in which the edges are a different color than the color of the main petals.

'Connecticut' African violet

'Kazuko' African violet

MOISTURE: African violet performs best if the soil is kept evenly moist. It is important to use only tepid water and to avoid getting water on the leaves. Drops of water, especially cold water, cause brown leaf spots. Avoid low humidity.

LIGHT: Medium light will give the best growth performance for this plant. However, high light makes the rosette flatten out, which can make an attractive backdrop to show off the flowers.

TEMPERATURE: Average to warm temperatures are best.

'Vermont' African violet

FERTILIZATION: Fertilize with a dilute solution every time the plants are watered using 10-30-10. If your plant is of the very common Optimara brand, bred by the Holtkamp family, it will require fertilizer designed for that brand; the nutrient ratio will be different than for other types.

PESTS: Watch for mealybugs and aphids on your African violet. Stem and crown rot can be problems in waterlogged soil and cool temperatures. If the flowers become distorted and somewhat discolored, suspect cyclamen mites or thrips.

REPOTTING: Repotting is only necessary if you want a plant to grow larger or if the plant becomes leggy or grows a "neck." The plant blooms best if slightly pot bound. Use a rich potting mix for flowering plants.

PROPAGATION: The most common method, because it is so easy with African violets, is to take leaf cuttings.

TIPS: Because African violet almost always consists of a rosette of leaves on a single stem, pruning is only needed to remove any unsightly leaves and spent blossoms.

Potting African violets: Gently lift the plant from the old pot, cradling its crown in your palm. Settle the plant into its new pot, still in your palm, and sift soil around the roots. Firm soil lightly, then remove your palm.

'Maine' African violet

SANSEVIERIA TRIFASCIATA

Snake Plant or Mother-in-Law's Tongue
Agavaceae

Native to arid Africa, snake plant is one of the most abused and most tolerant house-plants. Stories abound about forgotten plants coming back to life immediately upon watering. The long, tonguelike leaves emerge from rhizomes, and you can leave a plant in a single pot for many years to become thick and lush-looking. The patterned markings on the leaves call to mind the markings of an exotic snake, which is where one of the common names comes from. A wide variety of cultivars is available, with cream, white, yellow, and lime green markings on leaves.

MOISTURE: Allow the soil to dry out slightly between waterings. Overwatering causes leaf and crown rot, which may not be revealed until a leaf collapses.

LIGHT: Although it will tolerate low light, snake plant will perform best in medium or high light.

TEMPERATURE: Thrives at most temperatures.

FERTILIZATION: Fertilize infrequently, perhaps once a year using 10-10-10.

PESTS: Mealy bugs and leaf rot are problems. Otherwise, the plant is pest free.

REPOTTING: Because of a much-reduced root system, repotting is seldom necessary. Use a cactus type mix—one that drains quickly and well.

PROPAGATION: Propagate by leaf cuttings or rhizome division. Variegated varieties do not reproduce true from leaf cuttings but only from rhizome divisions.

TIPS: Although sansevieria has a reputation of being very tolerant of a wide range of cultural conditions, if you give it some extra attention, you can keep the plant in top form. Prune out leaves selectively if they become damaged. Leaving a scarred leaf will only detract from the plant's overall appearance. Plant many in one pot for the best look.

Snake plant

SAXIFRAGA STOLONIFERA

Strawberry Begonia
Saxifragaceae

Not a begonia at all, the strawberry begonia gets its name from its habit. The rounded, silver-veined leaves emerge on red petioles from the crown. The plant produces trailing stolons that bear tiny plantlets resembling the parent plant. All of the leaves are tinged with red on the undersides, and the plant makes a stunning, delicate plant in a hanging basket. The cultivar 'Tricolor', smaller than others of the species, has leaves of bright green and white, with the white turning soft pink if grown in proper light. In good light, the plants send up spikes of white starry flowers.

MOISTURE: Keep the soil evenly moist during its active growth. Reduce watering in winter, giving it just enough to keep the potting mix from drying out completely. Keep the humidity high if the plant is grown at temperatures above 65° F.

LIGHT: Medium to bright light is best for the most vivid coloring. 'Tricolor' benefits from some early morning sun.

TEMPERATURE: Provide average to cool temperatures.

Strawberry begonia

FERTILIZATION: Fertilize monthly during the active growing season using 10-10-10.

PESTS: Mealybugs and spider mites.

REPOTTING: Repot annually in a well-drained, average potting mix.

PROPAGATION: Clip the plantlets and pot them up.

TIPS: Start new plants regularly as old plants become rangy looking. Because the stolons are delicate, place the plant away from traffic.

Seasonal Cacti

The three common seasonal cacti are in actuality epiphytic cacti that are native to the rain forests of Brazil and southern Mexico. They are members of the cactus family but do not resemble cactus at all, nor are they used to the conditions of arid cactus.

All seasonal cactus have flattened, jointed stems that droop. Periodically, the plants fairly explode with blossoms.

These cacti have been highly hybridized, and the colors and shapes of flowers from which to choose are endless. They have a strong reputation as spectacular plants for hanging baskets.

MOISTURE: Allow the top 2 inches of soil to dry out between waterings. Keep drier in winter. Pay close attention to watering when the plant has flower buds—even slight dehydration or overwatering may cause bud drop.

LIGHT: Provide medium to high light.

TEMPERATURE: Average temperatures will suit during most of the year, but temperatures below 55° F in fall are required to initiate flower bud formation.

FERTILIZATION: Fertilize three times in summer or with a dilute solution at every watering using 10-30-10.

PESTS: Watch for aphids and mealybugs. Stem rot may be a problem if the plant is kept too wet.

REPOTTING: Repotting is only necessary if the plants become top-heavy. Use a coarse, fast-draining mix, such as one that's suitable for orchids.

PROPAGATION: Propagate by stem cuttings.

TIPS: To initiate flower buds, move your plants outdoors to a shaded spot in summer and leave them out as temperatures fall. Move them

'Madonga' Christmas cactus

Easter cactus

indoors before temperatures reach 45° F. To prune, pinch off stem segments where necessary to keep the plant shrubby.

TYPES OF SEASONAL CACTUSES

ORCHID CACTUS (*Epiphyllum Ackermannii*) This cactus sends out 2-foot or longer stems from a central crown and bears heart-breakingly beautiful, ethereal flowers that may be up to 9 inches across. The blooms can appear anywhere along the stems, from spring into early summer. Flowers range from dark red to yellow to white to purple to multicolored. During the summer, orchid cactus can be put outside in a moderately shaded location.

EASTER CACTUS (*Rhipsalidopsis gaertneri*) Easter cactus is so named because of its propensity to bloom in early spring (and sometimes again in early fall if conditions are right). The stems are softly scalloped, and on the tips are borne bell-shaped flowers with pointed, lilylike petals in all colors. Pink and red are common colors available in cultivars.

CHRISTMAS CACTUS (*Schlumbergera* × *buckleyi*) This plant, in its native South America, often grows on trees. Christmas cactus produces abundant flowers at the ends of the horned stems and most often blooms around Christmastime. The long, tubular blossoms with reflexed petals and contrasting stamens look like one flower tucked into another. The stems are bright green. Iridescent shades of red, purple, salmon, white, and multicolors grace these seasonal favorites. Christmas cactus looks particularly attractive when stems are pinched at different lengths, giving an almost multilayered look.

SOLEIROLIA SOLEIROLII

Baby's Tears

Urticaceae

Few gardeners can resist a sweet pot of tiny baby's tears. This softly mounding plant is native to the Mediterranean islands and is an incredibly tough plant that deceptively appears delicate. The small, round, olive leaves are borne along pinkish succulent stems. The stems break easily, which doesn't seem to make any difference to the beauty of the plant. Baby's tears can be used as ground-cover plants.

MOISTURE: Keep the soil evenly moist.
LIGHT: Bright filtered light will produce the best-looking plants, but baby's tears will tolerate almost any type of growing situation.
TEMPERATURE: Average is best.
FERTILIZATION: Fertilization is seldom necessary. When it is, use 10-10-10.
PESTS: Seldom bothered by pests.
REPOTTING: Annually, however, it's often easier to start new plants than to repot. Use average, well-drained mix.
PROPAGATION: Propagate by separating clumps and placing them on top of moist potting soil.
TIPS: This is a vigorous plant, so if you intend to use it as a ground cover, make sure you combine it with another sturdy plant so it doesn't engulf the larger plant. Pinch and prune as necessary to keep the plant aesthetically pleasing.

Baby's tears

SPATHIPHYLLUM WALLISII

Peace Lily

Araceae

Peace lily is commonly used in commercial settings because it tolerates most conditions and is low maintenance. In spite of being common, it is a beautiful low-light plant. It has dark green, glossy leaves with a slightly wavy edge, and white spathes, which contrast well with the leaves.

MOISTURE: Allow to dry out only slightly between waterings if the plant is kept in low light. In higher light, keep the soil evenly moist. Peace lily tolerates low humidity.

Peace lily

LIGHT: Does well in low light, but tends not to grow much. If you want the plant to put on new growth, give it medium light. Too much light inhibits bloom.
TEMPERATURE: Average temperatures are best. Cool temperatures increase chances of crown rot.
FERTILIZATION: Fertilize three times in summer using 10-10-10.
PESTS: Seldom a problem, but keep an eye out for mealybugs, spider mites, and crown rot.
REPOTTING: Seldom necessary. Can stay in the same pot for years. Pot in an average, well-drained soil.
PROPAGATION: Divide the crown.
TIPS: Pinch flowers as soon as they fade. Otherwise, the only pruning needed is an occasional leaf removal. Dust the leaves often; dust shows easily on the leaves.

STREPTOCARPUS X HYBRIDUS

Cape Primrose

Gesneriaceae

Cape primrose is a beautiful relative of African violets. Its long, narrow leaves are olive to dark green and covered with fine hairs. Each leaf, in actuality a plant in itself, sends up flower stalks that look like delicate wires covered with tube- or funnel-shaped flowers of blue, red, white, pink, or purple. Because it thrives in the same conditions as African violets, they are logical companions.

MOISTURE: Allow the soil to dry slightly between waterings. (Leaf tip dieback occurs if the soil dries too much.) Use tepid water and don't let any get on the leaves. Provide extra humidity with pebble trays or a humidifier.

LIGHT: Medium light is fine.
TEMPERATURE: Will tolerate warm temperatures, but performs best in cooler situations, especially with cool roots.
FERTILIZATION: Fertilize with a dilute solution every time you water using 10-30-10.
PESTS: Mealybugs and thrips.
REPOTTING: Seldom necessary. Pot in an average, well-drained soil.
PROPAGATION: Stem or leaf cuttings, divide rhizomes or grow from seed.
TIPS: Cape primrose readily sets seed capsules, so you can easily propagate by seeds. Prune only to remove spent flowers and selectively shape the plant after flowering. Cut the flower stalks rather than pulling them, which may pull off the leaf. Older leaves yellow and die.

Cape primrose

Succulents

Succulents represent a group of plants that have leaves unlike those of any other plants. They are thick and waxy and filled with water. This adaptation helps conserve moisture, often scarce in the plant's native habitat.

Window plant

MOISTURE: Because succulents can store moisture, the soil should be allowed to dry slightly between waterings. Overwatering often causes rotting. Water very little during the dormant season. Humidity levels are best kept low.

LIGHT: Provide medium to high light for succulents.

TEMPERATURE: Average to high, with cool temperatures in winter.

FERTILIZATION: Fertilize three times in summer using 10-10-10.

PESTS: Mealybugs and scales are occasional problems.

REPOTTING: Pot in a coarse, fast-draining mix. Repotting is seldom necessary.

PROPAGATION: Propagate by removing offsets and potting them.

TIPS: Pruning is seldom necessary. They are easily scarred; keep them out of traffic areas.

Hen and chicks

TYPES OF SUCCULENTS

HEN AND CHICKS (*Echeveria elegans*) The spoon-shaped leaves of hen and chicks form an almost flat rosette, about 4 inches in diameter, and produce attractive pink and yellow flowers in summer. When mature, the plant produces plantlets on long stolons that emerge from under the rosette. Plants are particularly prone to overwatering problems. If the plant fills the pot, water from below to avoid getting water on foliage, which can scar it.

WINDOW PLANT (*Haworthia tessellata*) This tiny succulent is usually brownish to green with a network of white veins. Provide medium light and avoid direct sun. Performs best without fertilizer and when water is withheld during their dormant period. Has bland, uninteresting flowers.

LIVING STONES (*Lithops* spp.) This oddity resembles stones rather than plants and often has mosaic markings of browns, pinks, and golds on its two leaves. In late summer a daisylike bloom appears from between the two leaves. It may remain solitary or develop into several clumps. Propagate by dividing a clump. It benefits from 3 to 4 hours of sun every day. Stop watering completely after bloom and until the new leaves emerge.

BURRO'S TAIL (*Sedum morganianum*) Burro's tail is a superb plant for use in a hanging basket. The stems trail up to 3 feet and are covered with overlapping gray-green to blue leaves. The leaves fall off easily, so remember to plant burro's tail where it will not be disturbed. It prefers full sun and no fertilization.

Living stones

Burro's tail

SYNGONIUM PODOPHYLLUM (NEPHTHYTIS)

Arrowhead Vine

Araceae

The native region of arrowhead vine ranges from Mexico all the way to Panama. The plant is related to the climbing philodendron. The lobed leaves are glossy green and deeply veined. As arrowhead vine matures, it begins to vine and can be easily trained onto a moss pole. It has aerial roots that will attach to a moist surface such as sphagnum moss.

MOISTURE: Arrowhead vine requires even watering, but allow the top inch of soil to dry out slightly between waterings. During its winter rest period, water only enough to keep the soil from drying out completely.

LIGHT: Bright light, but no direct sunlight.

TEMPERATURE: Average temperatures are best. If the temperature is higher than average, increase the humidity by using a pebble tray.

FERTILIZATION: Fertilize three times in summer. Fertilizing more often will cause the plant to grow rapidly.

PESTS: Mealybugs and spider mites are problems.

REPOTTING: Arrowhead vine performs best in an average, well-drained potting mix. Repot only as the roots fill the pot and as long as you want arrowhead vine to continue growing. When the desired size is reached, merely add about an inch or so of new soil each year.

Arrowhead vine

PROPAGATION: Propagate arrowhead vine by tip cuttings.

TIPS: Arrowhead vine rarely needs pruning except to remove an occasional damaged leaf. Although mature plants can be trained onto a pole, an immature plant is attractive when allowed to drape gracefully on a pedestal or flow from a hanging basket.

TOLMIEA MENZIESII

Piggyback Plant

Saxifragaceae

The piggyback plant is fairly common and is a beautiful addition to the indoor garden. It has a wonderful habit of producing baby plants in the center of each leaf. The medium green leaves are somewhat heart-shaped, with shallow lobes and deep veins. The leaf stalks and leaves are covered with soft hairs. Native to western North America, it tolerates a fairly wide range of temperatures.

MOISTURE: Allow the potting soil to dry out slightly between waterings.

LIGHT: Provide medium to bright light but no direct sunlight.

TEMPERATURE: Average temperatures will produce attractive specimens, although the plant is adaptable to a wide range of temperatures.

FERTILIZATION: Fertilize the plant three times in summer.

PESTS: Mealybugs and spider mites may be problems. Using a pebble tray will help to prevent spider mites.

REPOTTING: Piggyback plant is most attractive and full when several are potted together. Use an average, well-drained potting mix and repot only when roots fill the pot. Rejuvenate the plant regularly by propagating new plants to replace the old ones.

PROPAGATION: Produce new plants by snipping leaves with the largest "piggies" and potting them in small pots. You can also place a small pot next to the parent plant and pin down a leaf with a plantlet. After the plantlet has rooted, snip the leaf stalk.

Piggyback plant

TIPS: When the plant is awash with baby plants, the leaves tend to droop gracefully because of the extra weight. This habit makes piggyback plant an excellent candidate for a hanging basket or pedestal. Tolmiea has leaves that are hard to dust; it stays at its best if placed under the shower regularly.

Clip leaves with plantlets on top of them; set firmly on moist potting soil.

TRADESCANTIA ALBIFLORA

Wandering Jew

Commelinaceae

Wandering Jew or inch plant is a common houseplant that is grown for its variegated foliage. The species originally was solid green, but there are a multitude of cultivars with white stripes, purple and white stripes, or completely sulfur yellow. This plant is native to South America but has been naturalized throughout North America. Grown primarily for its foliage, wandering Jew seldom blooms indoors. Some of the most attractive

'Albovittata' wandering Jew

cultivars of the species are 'Albovittata', 'Aurea', and 'Tricolor'.

MOISTURE: Keep the soil evenly moist.

LIGHT: Provide bright light with some direct sunlight every day to help keep the leaves in top color.

TEMPERATURE: Average to high temperatures are best. Temperatures below 50° F will harm the plant.

FERTILIZATION: Fertilize three times in summer using 10-10-10.

PESTS: Mealybugs may occasionally be a problem.

REPOTTING: Pot in a rich, organic soil, and repot only as the plant fills the pot with roots. As the plant ages, it tends to become shabby, so begin new plants regularly to replace the old ones.

PROPAGATION: Propagate by tip cuttings. These are so easy to propagate that they can be rooted in water.

TIPS: The plant's trailing habit makes it an ideal candidate for a hanging basket. This plant also makes an attractive ground cover for larger houseplants. Pinch the tips occasionally to keep the plant bushy and full. Start a new plant directly in the pot with the mother plant to keep it looking full and healthy. This plant will need regular grooming to remove dead leaves.

TRADESCANTIA ZEBRINA

Purple Wandering Jew

Commelinaceae

Although this plant has the same common name as Tradescantia, the habit is a bit different. The stems are also trailing, but they are much thinner, and the leaves are spread out farther along the stem. The oval, pointed leaves are shimmering green and white on the upper sides and royal purple on the undersides. The plant produces clusters of small, white, three-petaled flowers in spring and summer. Native to Mexico and Guatemala, this plant is

Purple wandering Jew

extremely adaptable to heat and is often used as an outdoor ground cover in the South.

MOISTURE: Allow the potting mix to dry out slightly between waterings; this produces the most vivid color.

LIGHT: High light. Plants grown in medium light will survive, but the stems tend to elongate, and the leaves turn pale.

TEMPERATURE: Average to hot.

FERTILIZATION: Fertilize three times in summer using 10-10-10.

PESTS: Mealybugs may appear sporadically.

REPOTTING: Pot in an average, well-drained potting mix. Repot only as the plant fills the pot with roots.

PROPAGATION: Tip cuttings of the plant root easily.

TIPS: Pinch out plant tips regularly to encourage bushiness. Old leaves tend to dry up, leaving the stems bare. A plant with many bare stems can be cut back severely to encourage new growth. Replacing old plants with newly rooted cuttings is a way to always have an attractive plant. Fill a hanging basket with many cuttings to get a full look. Purple and green wandering Jews make excellent companions. Put cuttings of both in the same pot for a colorful combination. Purple wandering Jew is also an attractive ground cover for large plants.

INDEX

Page numbers in italics denote photographs; boldface numbers refer to Directory of Houseplants entries.

METRIC CONVERSIONS

U.S. Units to Metric Equivalents			Metric Units to U.S. Equivalents		
To Convert From	Multiply By	To Get	To Convert From	Multiply By	To Get
Inches	25.4	Millimeters	Millimeters	0.0394	Inches
Inches	2.54	Centimeters	Centimeters	0.3937	Inches
Feet	30.48	Centimeters	Centimeters	0.0328	Feet
Feet	0.3048	Meters	Meters	3.2808	Feet
Yards	0.9144	Meters	Meters	1.0936	Yards
Square inches	6.4516	Square centimeters	Square centimeters	0.1550	Square inches
Square feet	0.0929	Square meters	Square meters	10.764	Square feet
Square yards	0.8361	Square meters	Square meters	1.1960	Square yards
Acres	0.4047	Hectares	Hectares	2.4711	Acres
Cubic inches	16.387	Cubic centimeters	Cubic centimeters	0.0610	Cubic inches
Cubic feet	0.0283	Cubic meters	Cubic meters	35.315	Cubic feet
Cubic feet	28.316	Liters	Liters	0.0353	Cubic feet
Cubic yards	0.7646	Cubic meters	Cubic meters	1.308	Cubic yards
Cubic yards	764.55	Liters	Liters	0.0013	Cubic yards

To convert from degrees Fahrenheit (F) to degrees Celsius (C), first subtract 32, then multiply by $\frac{5}{9}$.

To convert from degrees Celsius to degrees Fahrenheit, multiply by $\frac{9}{5}$, then add 32.